ENGLISH in Common 6A

Student Book/Workbook
with ActiveBook

JJ Wilson with Antonia Clare

Series Consultants
Sarah Louisa Birchley and María Victoria Saumell

ALWAYS LEARNING

PEARSON

English in Common 6A
Student Book/Workbook Split Edition

Pearson Education, 10 Bank Street, White Plains, NY 10606

Staff credits: The editorial, design, production, and manufacturing people who make up the *English in Common 6* team are Margaret Antonini, Allen Ascher, Rhea Banker, Eleanor Kirby Barnes, Peter Benson, Mike Boyle, Tracey Cataldo, Aerin Csigay, Mindy DePalma, Dave Dickey, Chris Edmonds, Mike Kemper, Jessica Miller-Smith, Laurie Neaman, Daria Ruzicka, Loretta Steeves, Jeff Zeter, and Charlie Green.

This series is dedicated to Charlie Green. Without Charlie's knowledge of pedagogy, strong work ethic, sense of humor, patience, perseverance, and creativity, *English in Common* would never have existed.

Cover design: Tracey Cataldo
Cover photo: © qushe/shutterstock.com
Text design: Tracey Cataldo
Text composition: TSI Graphics
Text font: MetaPlus

ISBN 13: 978-0-13-262907-2
ISBN 10: 0-13-262907-0

Library of Congress Cataloging-in-Publication Data
Bygrave, Jonathan
English in common. Book 1 / Jonathan Bygrave.
p. cm.
ISBN 0-13-247003-9—ISBN 0-13-262725-6—
ISBN 0-13-262727-2—ISBN 0-13-262728-0—
ISBN 0-13-262729-9—ISBN 0-13-262731-0
1. English language—Textbooks for foreign speakers.
2. English language—Grammar.
3. English language—Spoken English.
PE1128.B865 2011
428.24--dc23

2011024736

Student Book Photos Credits: All photos are used under license from Shutterstock.com except for the following: Page 7 (B) Corbis Bridge/Alamy; p. 8 (left) Aurora Photos/Alamy, (right) Jonathan Littlejohn/Alamy; p. 11 (background) Image Source Ltd. www.imagesource.com, (top) GL Archive/Alamy; p. 12 (top right) iStockphoto.com; p. 15 (top) AFP/Getty Images/Newscom, (bottom) AFP/Getty Images/Newscom; p. 24 Zumapress.com/Newscom; p. 26 (top) Dreamstime.com; p. 31 (A) World History Archive/Alamy, (B) North Wind Picture Archives/Alamy, (C) Moviestore collection Ltd/Alamy, (D) iStockphoto.com; p. 32 (top) Bettmann/Corbis, (bottom) Lane Stewart/Sports Illustrated/Getty Images; p. 38 United Archives GmbH/Alamy; p. 39 (right) Moviestore collection Ltd/Alamy; p. 44 AF archive/Alamy; p. 45 (top) AF archive/Alamy, (bottom) Photos 12/Alamy; p. 52 (top) AP Images/Wong Maye-E, (bottom) Photo by Jun Takagi; p. 54 (top right) Spencer Platt/Getty Images; p. 55 (C) Stringer/Reuters/Corbis; p. 58 (right) iStockphoto.com; p. 61 (top) Pictorial Press Ltd/Alamy, (bottom) J.P. Moczulski/X01779/Reuters/Corbis; p. 72 AFP/Getty Images/Newscom

Workbook Photo Credits: All photos are © Pearson Education except for the following. Workbook p. 4 Simon Fergusson/Getty Images; Workbook p. 6 Shutterstock.com; Workbook p. 7 Shutterstock.com; Workbook p. 9 Shutterstock.com; Workbook p. 12 (all) Shutterstock.com; Workbook p. 16 (left) Peter Horree/Alamy, (top right) Sami Sarkis Travel/Alamy, (bottom right) Shutterstock.com; Workbook p. 17 Shutterstock.com; Workbook p. 19 Shutterstock.com; Workbook p. 20 Shutterstock.com; Workbook p. 22 Shutterstock.com; Workbook p. 27 Shutterstock.com; Workbook p. 28 (left) AF archive/Alamy, (right) Photos 12/Alamy, (bottom) AF archive/Alamy; Workbook p. 30 Shutterstock.com; Workbook p. 32 Ami Vitale/Getty Images; p. 36 Shutterstock.com; p. 37 Shutterstock.com; Workbook p. 43 Shutterstock.com.

Illustration Credits: Beach (Beach-o-matic), Mark Duffin, Brian Lee, Sally Newton, Amanda Montgomery-Higham (SGA), Roger Penwill, and Lucy Truman (New Division)

Text Credits: Page 15, "Brazilian Racing Star" from "Mirror, signal, manoeuvre" by Matt Rendell from *The Observer*, May 9, 2004. Copyright © 2004 by Guardian News & Media Ltd. Reprinted by permission of the Guardian News & Media Ltd. Page 44, "How to Be a Superhero" from "Special Report: Superhero Science" by Caroline Green from *Focus Magazine*, August 2004, #141. Reprinted by permission of author. Page 46, Audio 1.17 from an interview with Stan Lee. Used by permission of Stan Lee. Page 58, Audio 1.23 from "Picking the right partner" by Cliff Ennico from www.entrepreneur.com, April 1, 2002. Reprinted by permission of Cliff Ennico.

Printed in the United States of America
2 2019

Contents

Student Book

Workbook

English in Common is a six-level course that helps adult and young-adult English learners develop effective communication skills that correspond to the Common European Framework of Reference for Languages (CEFR). Every level of *English in Common* is correlated to a level of the CEFR, and each lesson is formulated around a specific CAN DO objective.

English in Common 6 has ten units. Each unit has twelve pages.

There are three three-page lessons in each unit.

A Unit Wrap Up ends each unit.

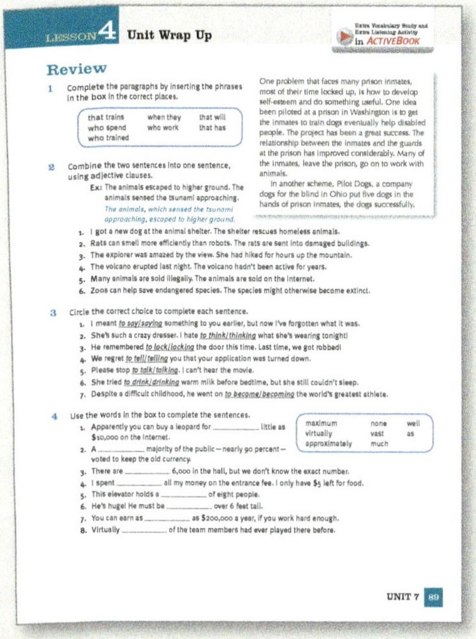

Back of Student Book

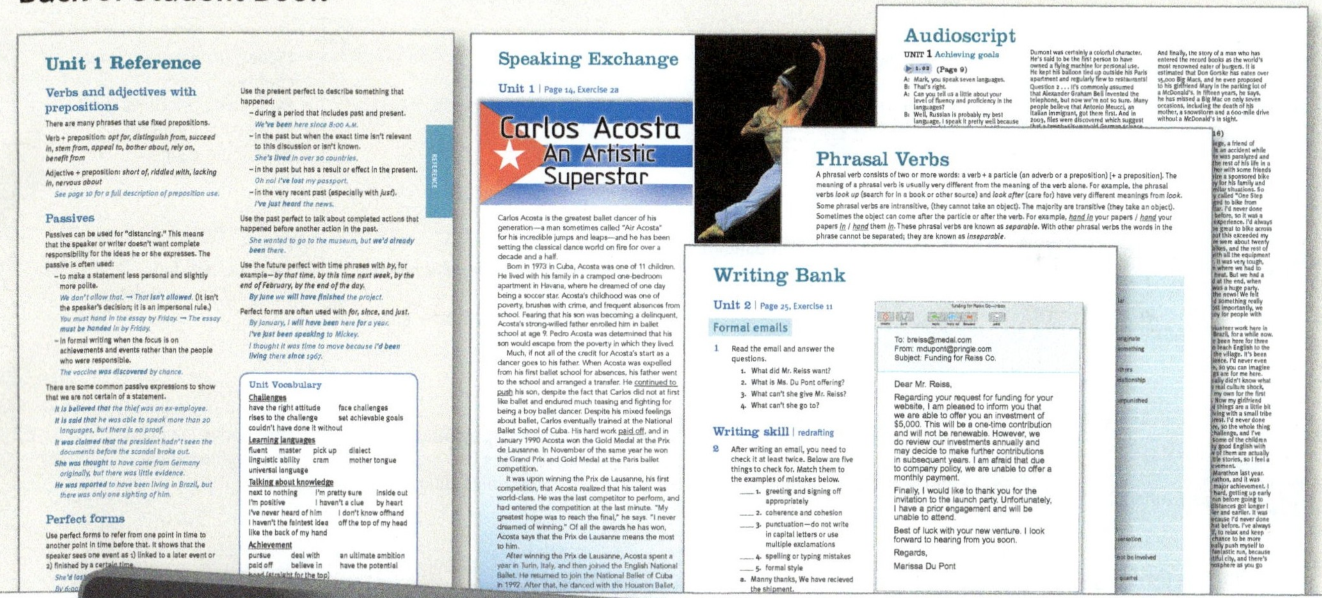

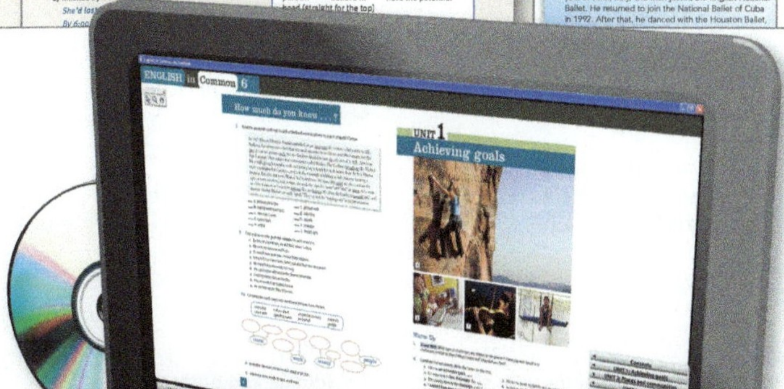

- Each Student Book contains an ***ActiveBook***, which provides the Student Book in digital format. *ActiveBook* also includes the complete Audio Program and Extra Listening activities.
- An optional online **MyEnglishLab** provides the opportunity for extra practice anytime, anywhere.
- The Teacher's Resource Book contains teaching notes, photocopiable extension activities, and an ***ActiveTeach***, which provides a digital Student Book enhanced by interactive whiteboard software. *ActiveTeach* also includes the videos and video activities, as well as the complete Test Bank.

READING/WRITING	LISTENING	COMMUNICATION/EXTRA VOCABULARY STUDY
Reading texts: • an article about polyglots • articles about two incredible athletes • a personality quiz **Writing task:** write a news report based on a picture	**Listening texts:** • an interview with a polyglot • a radio show about "famous firsts" • news stories • descriptions of personal achievements • analysis of answers to a personality quiz	**Communication:** take a personality quiz **Extra Vocabulary Study in *ActiveBook*:** prefixes
Reading texts: • an article about Wikipedia • formal emails • descriptions of travel destinations **Writing tasks:** • write recommendations for travelers to your country • write a formal email • write a description of a favorite place	**Listening texts:** • descriptions of life abroad • a debate over the value of the Internet • descriptions of two clubs to which people belong	**Communication:** collaborate on a plan **Extra Vocabulary Study in *ActiveBook*:** phrasal verbs
Reading texts: • an article about famous hoaxes • a biography of Groucho Marx **Writing task:** write a description of someone	**Listening texts:** • descriptions of favorite fictional characters • an abridged biography of Groucho Marx • a joke	**Communication:** tell a story **Extra Vocabulary Study in *ActiveBook*:** metaphors
Reading texts: • an article on scientifically generated "superpowers" • an article on child geniuses • descriptions of new technology **Writing task:** summarize a story from a listening	**Listening texts:** • news stories • a conversation about superheroes • an interview with the creator of Spider Man • telephone conversations about future plans • an interview about child geniuses • discussions about discoveries and inventions	**Communication:** make an argument for research funding **Extra Vocabulary Study in *ActiveBook*:** two-part expressions
Reading texts: • an article about a unique business model • true "riches to rags" stories • an article about famous philanthropists • an article about *Fortune* Magazine's 100 Best Companies to Work For **Writing task:** write a paragraph supporting an opinion	**Listening texts:** • advice on choosing a business partner • an interview with the CEO of a successful company • a discussion about a hypothetical business situation	**Communication:** negotiate **Extra Vocabulary Study in *ActiveBook*:** idioms 1
Reading texts: • an article on architecture as a symbol of power • an article about the power of charisma **Writing tasks:** • write about two important pieces of architecture • write an autobiographical statement	**Listening texts:** • descriptions of important architectural structures • an interview about the influence of teens on technology • conversations about limits on teenagers	**Communication:** evaluate personal characteristics **Extra Vocabulary Study in *ActiveBook*:** idioms 2
Reading texts: • an article on using animals to save human lives • an article about illegal online animal sales **Writing tasks:** • explain procedures in your home • write an ad for an object	**Listening texts:** • advice on choosing and caring for pets • a description of a travel adventure • a description of an unusual job • a discussion about how to develop a piece of land	**Communication:** reach a compromise on a plan **Extra Vocabulary Study in *ActiveBook*:** suffixes
Reading texts: • opinions on necessary future inventions • an "online" advice column **Writing tasks:** • write an essay on a problem or issue	**Listening texts:** • descriptions of imaginary inventions • explanations of career choices • conversations about problems with machines	**Communication:** summarize opinions on issues **Extra Vocabulary Study in *ActiveBook*:** academic English
Reading texts: • an article about famous visionaries • an article about fine art theft • advice for aspiring travel writers and photographers **Writing tasks:** • write about thoughts and actions inspired by a photo • write a story based on a hypothetical situation	**Listening texts:** • an interview about geniuses' "aha" moments • conversations about works of art • histories of two important inventors	**Communication:** collaborate on a proposal **Extra Vocabulary Study in *ActiveBook*:** confusing words
Reading texts: • an article about a blind photographer • a book review • an excerpt from a novel **Writing task:** write about a childhood memory	**Listening texts:** • an interview about optimism and pessimism • deductions about feelings in the past • recollections of childhood • explanations of strong opinions	**Communication:** express strong feelings about an issue **Extra Vocabulary Study in *ActiveBook*:** phrasal verbs and particles

How much do you know . . . ?

1 Read the paragraph and match each underlined word or phrase to a part of speech below.

In 1967 Allen and Beatrice Gardner embarked on an experiment (**1.**) to train a chimpanzee to talk. Realizing that chimpanzees don't have the vocal apparatus to be able to speak like humans, but that they (**2.**) can use gestures easily (**3.**), the Gardners decided to train the (**4.**) animal in ASL, American Sign Language. Their subject was a chimpanzee called Washoe. The Gardners brought up (**5.**) Washoe like a child, giving her regular meals and getting her to brush her teeth before sleep. At first, Washoe made meaningless hand gestures, similar to the meaningless babbling of baby humans learning a language. But after four years, Washoe had learned over 150 signs. She could (**6.**) also combine the signs on some occasions, such as when she made the signs for "water" and "bird" on seeing (**7.**) a swan on a lake. Linguists and scientists, however (**8.**), are skeptical (**9.**) about the Gardners' research (**10.**), and question whether Washoe can really "speak." They say that her "language use" is simply imitation.

____ **a.** gerund
____ **b.** linking word (contrast)
____ **c.** non-count noun
____ **d.** count noun
____ **e.** article
____ **f.** phrasal verb
____ **g.** adjective
____ **h.** adverb
____ **i.** pronoun
____ **j.** modal verb

2 Find and correct the grammar mistake in each sentence.

1. By this time tomorrow, we will have arrive in Peru.
2. We were hot because we'd run.
3. If I would have seen you, I would have stopped.
4. It mustn't have been John; John's tall and that man was short.
5. We haven't been knowing her long.
6. The conference will held in the theater tomorrow.
7. I had my purse stole yesterday.
8. She persuaded me buying the car.
9. He climbed up the Mount Everest.

3a Complete the word maps with words and phrases from the box.

step-sister	culture shock	uncharted territory	soulmate
career path	spending spree	be laid off	gamble

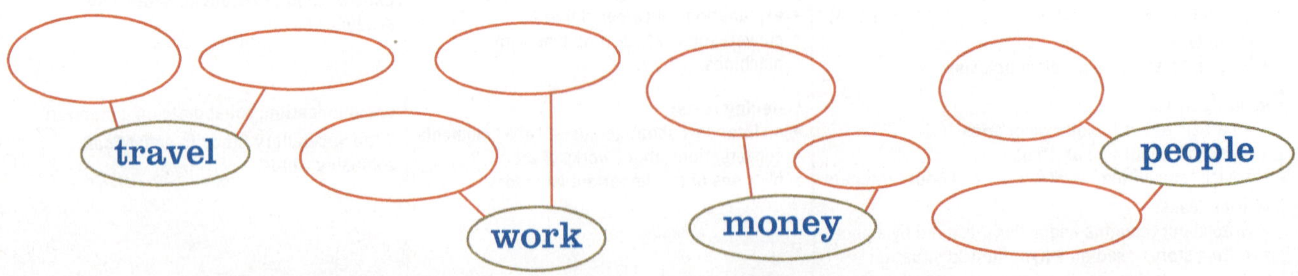

b Underline the main stress in each word or phrase.

c Add three more words to each word map.

UNIT 1
Achieving goals

Warm Up

1 **Group Work** What type of challenges are shown in the photos? Have you ever faced any challenges similar to these? What happened? How did you feel?

2 Complete the sentences. Write the letter on the line.

1. I like to **set achievable goals,** ____
2. It's important to **face challenges,** but ____
3. She usually **rises to the challenge,** even if ____
4. I **couldn't have done it without** help, so ____
5. It's important to **have the right attitude,** because ____

a. I'd like to thank my family and my sponsors.
b. so before starting, I always think about my objectives.
c. if you are a positive person, it will be easier.
d. you mustn't be afraid of them.
e. it's something very difficult.

3 **Pair Work** Discuss. What are your goals for your career or your personal life? What challenges do you think you will face in achieving these goals?

LESSON 1

Discuss your language learning experiences

GRAMMAR verbs and adjectives with prepositions

CAN DO

Reading

1 **Pair Work** How many languages do you speak? When did you learn them?

2a Read about some amazing language learners.

Great Language Learners

1 Cardinal Giuseppe Mezzofanti (1774–1849), who spoke 72 languages, is said to have once learned a language overnight in order to hear the confession of two condemned prisoners the following morning. Modern linguists laugh at this story, but they admit that there are some phenomenal polyglots out there.

2 The greatest is probably Francis Sommer. Sommer, who grew up in Germany and died in 1978, was fluent in 94 languages. He began learning languages as a young boy, starting with Swedish, Sanskrit, and Persian. He went on to master all of the major European languages as well as languages from other parts of the world. David Perlmutter, Professor of Linguistics at the University of California, says, "People like Sommer are amazing examples of human achievement."

3 Another great polyglot is Kenneth Hale, a linguistics professor who speaks roughly 50 languages. "I didn't do very well as a student," he says. "I wanted to learn languages, and I let everything else slide." Hale says that he and other master linguists learn languages not for money or recognition but for the pleasure that comes with mastering each new language. "When I found I could speak Navajo at the age of 12," says Hale, "I used to go out every day and sit on a rock and talk Navajo to myself."

4 Some studies suggest that people with a talent for languages may actually have a slightly different brain structure than the rest of us. Polyglots may have more white brain matter, which is involved in connecting different parts of the brain together. Faster language learners have more white brain matter in the area of the brain where sound is processed, which could result in an increased ability to process sound.

5 Stephen Wurm, linguistics professor at the Australian National University at Canberra, speaks 48 languages. He believes the best way to learn a language is to hear it spoken regularly from a very early age. Wurm's parents and grandparents, each of whom came from a different part of the world, spoke different languages with him when he was a child. His father spoke to him only in English, his mother in Hungarian, and his grandparents in Norwegian, Finnish, and Mongolian. Wurm also traveled with his father, who worked in Germany, Russia, China, Argentina, and Turkey, so he picked up those languages as well. He recalls, "By the age of six, I spoke ten different languages."

6 The greatest of today's polyglots is Ziad Fazah. Fazah, a Lebanese in his 50s who has been living in Brazil for over 20 years, is fluent in 56 languages. In addition to Arabic, his mother tongue, he learned French and English as a child. After that, Fazah taught himself German, then Mandarin Chinese, Cantonese, and Japanese, and on and on. He says that Mandarin was the most difficult language to learn.

7 Fazah teaches several languages, including English, Arabic, Farsi, French, and German. In addition, Fazah's abilities have had some unexpected uses. Several years ago, police in Rio called him to help with an illegal immigrant who spoke a language that they could not recognize. "I soon realized he was from Afghanistan and spoke a dialect called Hazaras," Fazah said.

8 TV fame also arrived unexpectedly. He appeared on TV shows in Spain and Greece, where his linguistic abilities were tested by people from Thailand, Hungary, Korea, Japan, China, and other countries. The US consulate in Brazil was less impressed, however. Because of his ability to speak Chinese and Russian, they feared he was a spy and asked the Brazilian police to bring him in for questioning. "After two hours I was let go," he says.

9 So do polyglots ever get their languages mixed up? Yes, says Kenneth Hale. He says that sometimes he starts speaking in one language but ends up speaking in a different one. He points out that if he's not paying attention, it's easy to mix up similar languages. Likewise, Francis Sommer stopped learning new languages in his old age, saying, "I am afraid to cram any more words into my head." Fazah, however, has room for at least one more language. He would like one day to create a new universal language that would be written as it is spoken.

b Now answer the questions.

1. Why do polyglots keep learning languages?
2. How might polyglots' brains be different from most people's brains?
3. What do polyglots sometimes worry about?
4. What positives and negatives has Ziad Fazah experienced because of his linguistic abilities?

3 **Pair Work** Discuss.

1. What are the benefits of being a polyglot? Are there any drawbacks?
2. In your opinion, what personal qualities are necessary to become a polyglot?

I think it would be amazing to be able to speak many languages. On the other hand . . .

Vocabulary | learning languages

4 Match the words and expressions from the Reading with the correct definitions.

____ 1. fluent (adj.)	a. put too much into a small space
____ 2. master [something] (v.)	b. level of skill in learning languages
____ 3. pick up [a language] (v.)	c. to learn something so well that you understand it completely
____ 4. mother tongue (n.)	d. able to speak a language very well
____ 5. dialect (n.)	e. the first language you learn
____ 6. linguistic ability (n.)	f. a form of a language that is spoken in one area
____ 7. cram (v.)	g. a language spoken by everyone
____ 8. universal language (n.)	h. to learn something without much effort

Listening

5a 1.02 Listen to Mark Sorok talk about his experiences as a language learner. Make notes about the following:

1. The number of languages he speaks
2. Special techniques he uses
3. How he feels about language

b Compare your notes with a partner. Listen again to check your answers.

6 **Pair Work** Discuss your own language learning experiences. What problems have you had? What do you like best about learning languages?

I learned to speak Portuguese when I was a child . . .

Grammar | verbs and adjectives with prepositions

7 Match the pictures with the sentences below.

____ 1. Marco found he was very short on opportunities to use his English.

____ 2. Tanya tended to rely on translation when she learned new words.

8 Read the rules and answer the questions in the Active Grammar box.

Active Grammar

1. There are many expressions that use a fixed preposition. Which sentence in Exercise 7 contains *verb + preposition*? ____________ Which contains *adjective + preposition*? ____________
2. Prepositions after verbs, nouns and adjectives always have an object. What is the object in each of the sentences in Exercise 7?

   1. ______________ 2. ______________
3. When the preposition is followed by a verb, the verb is usually a gerund.

   *I look forward to **meeting** you.* *She apologized for **taking** the camera.*

See Reference page 67

9 Add the correct prepositions from the box to each sentence. Check any new expressions in your dictionary.

from (x3)	to	in (x2)
about	for	with (x2)

1. Do you think you'll succeed ____________ passing your next test?
2. If you could improve your English by watching DVDs, living in an English-speaking country, or studying from books, which would you opt ____________?
3. Do your problems in English stem ____________ poor grammar, or are there other problems?
4. Do you feel you are lacking ____________ opportunities to practice speaking?
5. Some students' spoken English is riddled ____________ errors. Do you think this matters, or is fluency more important?
6. What distinguishes your first language ____________ English?
7. What types of classroom exercises appeal ____________ you?
8. Do you think pronunciation is worth bothering ____________?
9. Are you nervous ____________ giving presentations in English?
10. How can your fluency benefit ____________ watching TV?

Speaking

10a **Pair Work** Ask and answer the questions in Exercise 9. Explain your answers.

Yes, I'm sure I'll pass my next test. I've studied a lot.

b Tell the class what you learned about your partner.

Say how much you know or don't know

CAN DO ✓

GRAMMAR passives

Vocabulary | talking about knowledge

1a Complete the sentences with words from the box.

nothing	sure	head
positive	hand	know
heart	clue	out
certain	idea	of

1. A: Who won the match last night?
___ B: **I haven't a** ________.
2. A: Who wrote *Silas Marner*?
___ B: **I don't know off the top of my** ________.
3. A: Which nation has the smallest population?
___ B: **I'm pretty** ________ it's the Vatican.
4. A: Where did Elisha Gray come from?
___ B: Who? **I've never heard** ________ **him.**
5. A: Do you know Paris?
___ B: Yes. I lived there for years, so **I know it like the back of my** ________.
6. A: When did a man first go to the Moon?
___ B: **I don't** ________ **offhand,** but I can look it up.
7. A: Do you know Eliot's poem about cats?
___ B: **I know it by** ________. I learned it at school.
8. A: What do you know about corporate law?
___ B: **I know it inside** ________. I have a Ph.D. in it.
9. A: What do you know about Belgian politics?
___ B: **I know next to** ________ about it.
10. A: Which country has the biggest population?
___ B: **I haven't the faintest** ________.
11. A: Are you sure Russia is the biggest country in the world?
___ B: **I'm fairly** ________ it is, but it might be China.
12. A: Are you sure Mt. Everest is the highest mountain in the world ?
___ B: Yes. **I'm** ________ it is.

b Think about the meaning of the expressions **in bold**.
Write ✓ next to the expressions that mean *I know*.
Write ✗ next to the expressions that mean *I don't know.*

Speaking

2 **Pair Work** Ask a partner how much they know or don't know about the topics in the box. Try to use the expressions from Exercise 1a.

Antonio Meucci	classical music
the World Cup	the North Pole
Alexander Graham Bell	computers
the history of flight	the Tango
Leonardo da Vinci	jazz
Isabel Allende	sports
global warming	sailing

Listening

3 **Pair Work** Take the quiz. If you disagree, discuss your answers. Use the vocabulary from page 11.

WHO DID IT FIRST?

1. Who was the first to fly a plane?
   a. Alberto Santos Dumont
   b. the Wright brothers
   c. Von Zeppelin
2. Who invented the telephone?
   a. Thomas Edison
   b. Alexander Graham Bell
   c. Antonio Meucci
3. Who first reached the North Pole?
   a. Peary
   b. Cook
   c. Amundsen
4. Who invented the light bulb?
   a. Edison
   b. Bell
   c. Leonardo da Vinci

5. Which country won the first World Cup (and hosted it)?
   a. Brazil
   b. Uruguay
   c. Germany
6. Which was the first country to allow women to vote?
   a. Switzerland
   b. New Zealand
   c. the United States
7. Who was the first woman to sail solo around the world?
   a. Ellen MacArthur
   b. Amelia Earhart
   c. Naomi James
8. Which country held the first Olympic Games?
   a. Italy
   b. France
   c. Greece

4 ▶1.03 Listen to the radio show to find answers to the quiz. Does anything surprise you?

Grammar | passives

5 Read the Active Grammar box and circle the correct answer to item 1.

Active Grammar

1. The passive is often used to show that a statement is ____.
   a. not our own opinion
   b. a personal opinion

   It is said that . . .

   It is believed that . . .

   It is claimed that . . .

2. If we aren't sure that the information is 100 percent true, we can use the passive to put "distance" between ourselves and the statement.

   He is said to be the richest man in England (but I don't know if this is accurate).

   He was thought to have left the country (but I'm not sure if this is true).

   Other verbs for "distancing":

   It appears/seems that . . . *It seems as if/though . . .*

See Reference page 67

6 Complete the sentences using passives and the verbs in bold.

Ex: People say that Edison invented more machines than anyone else in history.

say *Edison* _*is said to have*_ *invented more machines than anyone else in history.*

1. The evidence suggests that Edison didn't invent as much as we thought.
   seems It ______________ though Edison invented fewer things than we thought.
2. People believe that da Vinci invented the helicopter.
   think Da Vinci ______________ invented the helicopter.
3. Some historians assert that the Wright brothers flew first.
   assert It ______________ by some historians that the Wright brothers flew first.
4. Many journalists in the late 19th century said that William Dickson had "invented" the motion picture in 1891.
   claim It ______________ that William Dickson had "invented" the motion picture.
5. We think Joop Sinjou and Toshi Tada Doi invented the CD player at the same time.
   believe Sinjou and Tada Doi ______________ invented the CD player simultaneously.
6. Newspapers of the time reported that Felix Hoffman had invented aspirin.
   report It ______________ that Felix Hoffman had invented aspirin.
7. We now think that aspirin was first used by ancient Egyptians.
   believe It ______________ that aspirin was first used by ancient Egyptians.

Listening

7a ▶1.04 Listen to the radio news headlines. Take notes on the stories you hear.

b **Pair Work** Retell the stories in your own words. Do you think these are important achievements? Discuss why or why not.

Speaking

8 **Pair Work** Look at the pictures and answer the questions.

1. Which story do you think is the most interesting? Why?
2. Which is the most likely or unlikely? Why?

I think the man who lived with lions is the most interesting because it seems impossible . . .

Writing

9a Write a news report based on one of the pictures in Exercise 8 (about 100–150 words). Use at least two passive constructions.

b **Group Work** Read your news reports to your classmates.

LESSON 3 Talk about your achievements

CAN DO

GRAMMAR perfect forms

Reading

1 **Pair Work** Discuss. Which sports are typically dominated by men? Which by women? Why do you think this is?

2a **Pair Work** Student A: read the article on page 15. Student B: read the article on page 72 in the Speaking Exchange. Make notes in the chart.

Name		
What is/was their ambition?		
To what extent have they achieved it?		
What challenges have they faced?		
Who has helped them achieve their ambitions? How?		

b Tell your partner about your article. What similarities are there between the two stories?

3 **Group Work** Discuss.

1. Carlos Acosta got teased for being a boy ballet dancer. Do you think that there is a prejudice that ballet is not for boys? Do you think it is the same in all countries?
2. What do you think of the fathers' behaviors in these two cases? Would you have reacted similarly? Do you believe that parents should influence the ambitions of their children?

Vocabulary | achievement

4a What do the following words and expressions from the articles mean? Use the context to help you establish the meaning.

1. head (straight for the top)
2. pursue (a dream)
3. deal with (chauvinism)
4. believe in (what you can achieve)
5. have the potential (to do something)
6. continue to push someone (to do something)
7. (something) paid off
8. an ultimate ambition

b Complete the sentences using the Vocabulary.

1. It was obvious that Venus Williams ________________ to become a tennis champion when she was very young.
2. Ralf Schumacher had to ________________ criticism from his colleagues.
3. Ellen MacArthur ________________ her dream of sailing solo around the world.
4. If you ________________ yourself, you can achieve almost anything.
5. Her ________________ is to be the best tennis player in the world.
6. Encourage your kids to try new things, but don't ________________ them too hard.
7. All of his hard work ________________ when he won the race.
8. That young singer is ________________ for the top.

Brazilian Racing Star

Meet Bia Figueiredo, who is set to join the ranks of her country's great racing drivers—Senna, Piquet, Barrichello. She has already beaten the boys from Brazil at their own game. Now she competes in the US, in the IZOD IndyCar series.

As the swarm of race cars completes its final warm-up lap and hurtles across the starting line, the race is on. Thirty minutes later, when the winner's helmet is removed, a wave of dense dark hair flows freely. For the champion is a girl, Ana Beatriz Figueiredo—Bia, for short—and she is heading straight for the top.

I first met Bia Figueiredo in May 2001. She was 16, and her rivals in São Paulo's kart scene—all male—had been suffering the obvious taunt for eight years: "Beaten by a girl . . . again?"

She is still winning. One day soon, the image of her long hair spilling out of her helmet could open motor sports to new audiences, sponsors, and perhaps a whole new lease of life. For as Bia pursues her dream, she is being spoken of as the possible future of racing, the woman to transform an increasingly predictable sport.

"The first time I went to the kartodrome," she tells me, "I was five or six. I begged my father to take me and fell in love with the noise and the crashes. He told me I had to be seven before I could learn to drive. Somehow I managed to wait."

Money pressures are inherent in motor racing, even for a family that is well-off by most standards. Compared with other drivers at this level, Bia is disadvantaged. Bia's father, Jorge, says that Bia was already dreaming of Formula 1 at the age of six. And having encouraged his daughter's passion, he has accepted the financial burden with good humor. "I once heard a Formula 1 team boss say it costs $10 million to become a Formula 1 driver. I said to myself, 'OK. I'm only $9,990,000 short!'"

Because of the expense, Bia could only do two 50-minute tests before each race, when other drivers did four. She went to one of the best schools in São Paulo, which meant she was doing school work when other drivers were on the track. "Given these constraints, she has done very well," her father says. "She was born with a forceful personality, and today she's still forceful and has a caustic sense of humor. I feel a little sorry for anyone in her way!"

Motor racing would not be every father's chosen career for his daughter. "Yes, it can be dangerous," Jorge concedes. "But the element of risk can be controlled. I'm much more afraid of Bia not doing what she loves. By pursuing what they enjoy, I think people have more chance of being happy."

Yet Bia will have to deal with chauvinism. Not the least of the barriers facing her is whether motor sports are prepared to accept a genuine female contender. "A beautiful woman is always welcome," Alex Dias Ribeiro says, smiling and then adds: "But she will have to be quick and mentally tough, because Formula 1 is a pressure cooker."

One man who believes in Bia's potential is her mechanic and mentor, Naylor Borigis de Campos, who is better known simply as Nô. Nô has worked closely with most of Brazil's best drivers. He compares Bia favorably with the best of his protégés. "She's as cool, aware, and determined as Rubens Barrichello and as any other driver I've ever worked with."

As for Bia herself, she believes in the future and in what she can achieve: "I have a lot to learn, but my temperament is right: I've got plenty of animal instinct. I believe I have the potential to reach Formula 1 and perhaps one day be a great driver."

Listening

5 **Pair Work** Talk about something you have done that was difficult. How did you prepare for it?

6 ▶1.05 Listen and answer the questions.

1. What has each person achieved?
2. What challenges did they face?

Grammar | perfect forms

7 Read the Active Grammar box. Match sentences a–c to the timelines on the right.

Active Grammar

Verbs used in their perfect forms link two times. The perfect aspect is used to refer back from one point to a point in time before that.

a. *Next week I'll have been here for three months.* (future perfect)

b. *My girlfriend has joined me.* (present perfect)

c. *I'd never done anything like that before.* (past perfect)

____ 1. Past and present

unspecified time in past — now

____ 2. Two points in the past

before that — past — now

____ 3. A point in the future

three months earlier — now — next week

Perfect continuous tenses, like other continuous tenses, focus on an event that continues or is temporary.

Next March ***I'll have been playing*** *with the team for five years.*

I've been doing *voluntary work all my adult life.*

See Reference page 67

8a Circle the correct choice.

1. Jake, this is my friend Amy, whom I've *been knowing/known* forever.
2. I asked what had *happened/been happened*, but nobody could tell me.
3. I chose this school because *I've heard/I'd heard* it was the best.
4. Before I came to the US, *I've/I'd* never been abroad.
5. I'm so exhausted. *I've/I'd* been working really hard.
6. By the time she retires, she'll *have been working/had been working* there for more than 50 years.

b ▶1.06 Listen and check your answers.

Speaking

9 **Pair Work** Think about your greatest achievement. Make notes using the language in the How To box. Then tell your partner. Try to use perfect verb forms in your story.

How To:

Talk about an achievement

Problems	• *I didn't know what to expect.* • *It was tough/a challenge.*
How it felt	• *It exceeded my expectations.* • *I felt like I'd accomplished something.* • *It was a great experience.*
Results/ follow up	• *I've learned a lot.* • *I'm looking forward to . . .*

LESSON 4 Unit Wrap Up

Extra Vocabulary Study and Extra Listening Activity in ActiveBook

Review

1 Complete the article with words from the box.

distinguished from	challenging	relied on	faced
benefited from	succeeded in	intelligible	pick up

The Hawaiian Creole language was invented through necessity. In 1880, thousands of immigrants from Europe and Asia went to work for the English-speaking owners of sugar plantations in Hawaii. Among all the other challenges these immigrants ________________ (1.), the most ________________ (2.) was to understand each other, to understand their bosses, and to understand the Hawaiian people. After a short time, they were able to ________________ (3.) some English, but barely enough to communicate. Instead, they ________________ (4.) body language and a simple code of sounds.

However, things changed fast, and by 1910 a new language had emerged: Hawaiian Creole. This included words and sounds from other languages, but it could be ________________ (5.) all of them by its different grammar. With this new easily understood language, everybody ________________ (6.) increased communication.

Many years later, Derek Bickerton studied the origins of Hawaiian Creole. He was amazed that within one generation, the immigrants had ________________ (7.) creating a language that was ________________ (8.) to all. In fact, in his book *Roots of Language*, he says that the children invented the language while playing together.

2 Add one word to each news headline to make it correct.

1. Sci-Corps Company seems to abandoned its research into cloning.
2. Former president Michael Nkrumah is said be recovering well from the stroke he suffered last Thursday.
3. The explorer Michaela Barker has been found in Brazil. It believed that she had drowned during a storm.
4. Baseball star Alex Hanai appears to finally retired at the age of 40.

3 Complete the sentences using a perfect form of the verb in parentheses.

1. By the time she finishes her degree, she ________________ (be) in school for ten years.
2. I feel healthier now that I ________________ (take up) kickboxing.
3. Where were you? I ________________ (wait) here for at least an hour!
4. I ________________ (run) for years before I entered my first marathon.
5. We ________________ (use up) all the world's oil long before 2100.

4 Put B's words in order to complete the conversations.

Ex: A: What is Pelé's real first name?
B: pretty I'm Edson it's sure. *I'm pretty sure it's Edson.*

1. **A:** Have you ever been to Prague?
   B: yes, I of the hand like my back it know ________________
2. **A:** How many women have succeeded in Formula 1 racing?
   B: I many know not but offhand, don't ________________
3. **A:** Can you help me with my homework? I need some information about space travel.
   B: know nothing it to next about I ________________
4. **A:** Who's Michael Vaughan?
   B: never him heard I've of ________________

Communication | take a personality quiz

5 **Pair Work** Complete the questionnaire. When you have finished, compare answers and think of another question to add.

DO YOU LIKE A CHALLENGE?

1. You are climbing a mountain with some friends. It is cold and wet, and you are halfway up. You ____.
   a. turn around and go home to a hot bath.
   b. keep going. Nothing will stop you once you've started.
   c. see what your friends want to do. It doesn't really matter if you reach the top.
2. You get an offer to work abroad for a year. It means you have to learn a diffcult new language and live in an isolated place with no nightlife. You ____.
   a. refuse politely. You'd have to be crazy to live in the middle of nowhere.
   b. accept. Who needs nightclubs? And you may love it.
   c. ask your colleagues, friends, and family what they think.
3. You are asked to perform in a local play. You will have to learn some lines and act in front of a large audience. You ____.
   a. say no. You aren't going to make a fool of yourself in public.
   b. jump up on stage and start singing. This is your chance at fame and fortune.
   c. ask exactly what you'll have to do, then think about it.
4. Your friends decide to learn to skydive. They want you to join them. You ____.
   a. refuse, saying you're too young to die.
   b. immediately book lessons. It'll be fun.
   c. find some statistics on the mortality rate of skydivers before committing yourself.
5. You are asked to cook for 15 people. You ____.
   a. immediately find out the name of a good caterer.
   b. start dreaming of the delicious feast you will prepare. It could be a great night.
   c. consult some cookbooks and figure out how much it will cost.
6. You are offered the chance to sail around the world. You ____.
   a. say no. You can't take the time off work.
   b. get ready to go immediately.
   c. ask for additional information before you commit.

6 ▶1.07 Listen to what your answers say about your personality.

7 **Pair Work** Discuss.

1. Which would be the most difficult challenge for you? Which would be the easiest? Why?
2. How would you prepare for each challenge?
3. Which do you think are harder—mental or physical challenges? Give examples.

Performing in a play would be the most difficult for me. I get really nervous speaking in front of large groups of people.

UNIT 2
Places and communities

A

B

C

D

Warm Up

1 **Pair Work** Discuss. What types of communities do the people in the photos belong to? What are the positive and negative aspects of each community?

2a Unscramble the underlined words and expressions and read the definitions. Then mark each item positive (+) or negative (–).

____ 1. reasonable octs of glinvi—not too expensive
____ 2. ldim climate—not extreme weather; not too hot or too cold
____ 3. personal ermefod—you are allowed to do what you want
____ 4. efficient ecraehalht system—plenty of good hospitals
____ 5. good addsarnt of ilgniv—you can have a good lifestyle
____ 6. high emcir reta—many crimes per year
____ 7. high level of pnmletouneym—many people don't have jobs
____ 8. ria ooitpulln—dirty air
____ 9. no utllruac life—lack of theaters, concert halls, art galleries, etc.
____ 10. vibrant ihilgfetn—many good nightclubs, restaurants, movie theaters

b **Pair Work** Discuss. Which four qualities from the list are the most important to you in a community? Why?

Personal freedom is really important to me. Also . . .

LESSON 1

Give advice and make recommendations about places

CAN DO

GRAMMAR gerund and infinitive review

Listening

1 **Pair Work** Discuss.

1. Have you ever lived abroad? Where? Describe your experience.
2. What problems might people living in a foreign country have?

2a ▶1.08 Listen to the descriptions of living abroad. Complete the chart.

	Speaker 1	Speaker 2	Speaker 3
1. Where did he or she live?			
2. What was he or she doing there?			
3. What did he or she like about the host country?			
4. Was there anything he or she didn't like or that was difficult?			
5. What are his or her favorite memories of the country?			

b Which of the speakers (1, 2, or 3):

____ 1. got a few surprises?

____ 2. was there at the wrong time?

____ 3. is from a small town?

____ 4. would like to return?

____ 5. learned about the culture by talking to the local people?

____ 6. says the place was multicultural?

____ 7. has lived in many countries?

____ 8. doesn't mention the scenery?

c Listen again to check your answers.

3 **Group Work** Discuss.

1. Which of the places in Exercise 2 would you most like to live in? Why?
2. Would you like to live abroad for a while? Why or why not?
3. Why do you think the speakers talk mainly about food, scenery, and people? Which of these do you think is the most important in a place?

Grammar | gerund and infinitive review

4 Complete the sentences. Use an infinitive or gerund and a **preposition** if necessary.

1. I'm **thinking** *of taking* ____ (take) a break.
2. If you can't **afford** ________ (eat) in expensive restaurants, Vancouver has many cheaper ones.
3. I can't **imagine** ________ (live) there.
4. You can **avoid** ________ (offend) people by learning the host country's customs.
5. I don't **mind** ________ (stand) in line.
6. She doesn't **want** ________ (miss out) on "fusion cuisine."
7. I can't **stand** ________ (travel).
8. If you **object** ________ (pay) lots of money, don't shop there.
9. I **encourage** all foreigners ________ (try) some real sushi.
10. I **urge** you ________ (see) Stanley Park in Vancouver.
11. I'd **recommend** ________ (go) to Tokyo Art Gallery.
12. She **persuaded** us ________ (visit) Austria in the spring.

5 Complete the Active Grammar box, using the verbs in bold in Exercise 4.

Active Grammar

Verb + gerund	Verb + infinitive	Verb + object + infinitive	Verb + preposition + gerund

See Reference page 68

6 Rewrite the sentences below, using a gerund or infinitive with the verb in bold. Begin each sentence with *I* or *I'm*.

Ex: You must go to the National Gallery. **urge** *I urge you to go to the National Gallery.*

1. I don't have the money to go to the theater. **afford**
2. You should go to the museum on Sunday. **advise**
3. I think people ought to use the parks more. **encourage**
4. You should buy tickets early. **recommend**
5. I never take the train. **avoid**
6. I may go to Thailand in February. **think**

7 **Pair Work** Think of a place you have visited. Make recommendations to your partner. Use some of the language in the How To box.

Toledo, Spain is a must-see. My favorite part is . . .

How To:

Give advice/make recommendations about places

Saying it's good	• *It's a must or a must-see.* • *It's a good value for the money.*
Saying it's not so good	• *It's a little bit overrated* or *overpriced.* • *It's not all it's cracked up to be.*
Recommending	• *If I were you, I'd go to . . .* • *Don't miss . . .* or *Make sure you go to . . .* • *You should try . . .*
Warning	• *Watch out for . . .*

Speaking

8 **Pair Work** Discuss.

1. What do you think "cultural awareness" means? Can you give any examples?
2. Do you think cultural awareness is important? Why or why not?
3. What cultural mistakes do foreigners sometimes make in your country?
4. Do you know of any customs or habits that are acceptable in your country but impolite in other countries?

9 Make the sentences more polite, using the words in the box.

please mind were was wondering think possible

1. Move your bag. → Would you __________ moving your bag?
2. Be quiet. → Could you __________ be a little bit quieter?
3. Slow down. → Do you __________ you could slow down a little?
4. I thought you could give us a ride. → I __________ hoping you could give us a ride.
5. Can you give me a hand? → I was __________ if you could give me a hand.
6. Can I get the room for two more nights? → Would it be __________ for me to get the room for two more nights?
7. You should stay in a small hotel. → If I __________ you, I'd stay in a small hotel.

10a **Pair Work** Have you ever made a mistake and offended someone from another culture without meaning to? Has someone from another culture ever unintentionally offended you? Discuss your experience. Answer these questions:

- Where were you? What happened?
- Did you (or the other person) realize at the time that a mistake had been made?
- What did you do to resolve the issue?

I was traveling in Indonesia for business last year. A colleague there asked me how much money I make. I was startled and said that that was private. I think I offended him—I didn't realize that it's common for people there to ask each other about their salaries. I later went back and apologized . . .

b Would you have made the same mistake as your partner? Why or why not?

11 **Group Work** Use your experiences from Exercise 10a to compile a "cultural awareness guide." Include advice on what people from your country should expect and how they should behave in other countries.

Writing

12 Write a "web page" with advice for visitors to your country. Include information on food, places to go, the best methods of transportation, holidays and festivals, and cultural advice. Use language from the How To box on page 21 and some of the verbs from the Active Grammar.

LESSON 2

Use features of formal and informal language

GRAMMAR comparisons

CAN DO

Listening

1 **Pair Work** Discuss.

1. How often do you use the Internet? What do you use it for?
2. Do you trust what you read on the Internet? Why or why not?

2 ▶1.09 Listen to the conversation. What issues do they discuss?

3 Listen again and check (✓) the phrases you hear.

____ 1. (It's) so much . . . (than)
____ 2. (It's) far . . . (than)
____ 3. (It's) not nearly as . . . as
____ 4. the less we . . . , the less we . . .
____ 5. the more we . . . , the more we . . .
____ 6. It's not quite as . . . as . . .
____ 7. It's considerably . . .
____ 8. It's slightly . . .
____ 9. (It's) almost the same as
____ 10. It's the same as
____ 11. It's a little bit . . . (than)

American English	British English
not nearly as . . .	*nowhere near as . . .*
so much (easier)	*miles (easier)*

Grammar | comparisons

4 Complete the chart in the Active Grammar box, using the phrases from Exercise 3.

Active Grammar

1. A big difference	
2. A little difference	
3. No difference	
4. *The* + comparative + *the* + comparative	

See Reference page 68

5 Complete the sentences with words or phrases from the Active Grammar box. Some items have more than one possible answer.

1. It's ____________ (easy) to communicate by email than by telephone.
2. Buying things in stores is ____________ as cheap as shopping online.
3. Writing on a computer is ____________ (fast) than writing by hand.
4. The more you use your smartphone, ____________ you will rely on it.
5. Buying things online is ____________ (risky) than face-to-face transactions.
6. Information on the Internet is not ____________ (reliable) as information in books.

Speaking

6 **Pair Work** Do you agree or disagree with the statements in Exercise 5? Discuss.

Reading

7 **Pair Work** Have you ever heard of or used Wikipedia? What is special about it?

8 Read the article. Then answer the questions below.

The Internet's largest encyclopedia

1 ______________________

Being the founder of the Internet's largest encyclopedia means Jimmy Wales gets a lot of strange emails. There are the correspondents who assume he wrote Wikipedia himself and is therefore an expert on everything—like the guy who found some strange chemicals in his late grandfather's attic and wanted Wales to tell him what to do with them. There are wackos who claim to have found, say, a 9,000-year-old, 15-foot human skeleton and wonder if Wales would be interested. But the emails that make him laugh out loud come from concerned newcomers who've just discovered they have total freedom to edit a Wikipedia entry at the click of a button. "Oh my gosh," they write, "you've got a major security flaw."

2 ______________________

Wikipedia is a free open-source encyclopedia, which means that anyone can log on and add to it or edit it. And they do. It has millions of entries in 281 languages—and counting. Academics are upset by what they see as info anarchy. A print encyclopedia editor once likened Wikipedia to a doorknob because you don't know who touched it last. But loyal users claim that collaboration improves articles over time.

3 ______________________

But what exactly is a wiki and how does it work? Wikis are deceptively simple pieces of software that you can download for free. You then use them to set up a website that can be edited by anyone you like. Need to solve a thorny business problem overnight and all the members of your team are in different time zones? Start a wiki. And the name? Believe it or not, the name came about because the inventor of the wiki had his honeymoon in Hawaii, where you catch the "wiki wiki" (quick) bus from the airport.

4 ______________________

Anyway, in 2001, Jimmy Wales was looking for a way to combine his two major hobbies: perusing the Encyclopedia Britannica and surfing the Internet. "I met all these great people online," he says, "and we were all discussing things on mailing lists no one ever looks at. I thought, why not build something more long-lasting, more fun and entertaining?"

5 ______________________

Ah, fun. Spend enough time talking to Wales—a confessed "pathological optimist"—and you'll believe his life has been one long riot of laughter. Options and futures trading, which he did in Chicago in the 1990s, was "fun and cool." Quitting his job to start an Internet company? Delightful. And Wikipedia's growth? Simply amazing.

6 ______________________

Wikipedia is the cumulative work of 16,000 people, the bulk of it done by a hard-core group of around 1,000 volunteers. Its over 3 million entries in English alone make it far larger than the Encyclopedia Britannica. And Wales pays just one employee, who keeps the servers ticking.

7 ______________________

Naturally there are many who take advantage of Wikipedia's open system to deface, delete, or push one-sided views. Sometimes extreme action has to be taken. For example, Wales locked the entries on John Kerry and George W. Bush for most of the 2004 presidential election campaign. But for the most part, such action is not necessary. According to an MIT study, obscene comments randomly inserted on Wikipedia are removed within 100 seconds, on average. Vandals might as well be spray-painting walls with disappearing ink.

8 ______________________

As for edit wars, in which two users with opposing views delete each other's assertions over and over, well, they're not much of a problem these days. All kinds of viewpoints co-exist in the same article. Take the entry on Wikipedia: "Wikipedia has been criticized for a perceived lack of reliability, comprehensiveness, and authority." Indeed, Larry Sanger, Wikipedia's former editor-in-chief (now a university professor), still loves the site but thinks his fellow professionals have a point. "The wide-open nature of the Internet encourages people to disregard the importance of expertise," he says. Sanger doesn't let his students use Wikipedia for their papers, partly because he knows they could confirm anything they like by adding it themselves.

1. What is Wikipedia?
2. What is a wiki?
3. Who is Jimmy Wales?
4. What problems has Wikipedia had?
5. What criticisms has it faced?
6. What do people like about it?

9 **Pair Work** Look at the How To box. Then discuss items 1–2.

1. Find other examples in the article of a) informal vocabulary, b) spoken English, and c) humor.
2. Are the following generally used in formal or informal texts: full verb forms, lots of phrasal verbs, sentences beginning with *and* or *but*, repeated use of the passive?

How To:

Recognize features of a colloquial writing style

Informal vocabulary	• *guy* (paragraph 1) • *wackos* (paragraph 1)
Spoken English style	• *say* (paragraph 1) • *Oh my gosh* (paragraph 1) • Short forms: *who've* (paragraph 1)
Omitted words	• *Need to solve a thorny business problem . . .* (paragraph 3). The full question = *Do you need to solve . . .* • *And the name?* (paragraph 3)
Humor	• *A print encyclopedia editor once likened Wikipedia to a doorknob because you don't know who touched it last.* (paragraph 2)

10 Read the two formal emails below. Some of the words and phrases used are too informal. Replace them with a more appropriate word or phrase from the box below.

will be very happy to attend	will be unable to attend	requested
we would be grateful if you could	a previous arrangement	concerning
could you please confirm your attendance	don't hesitate to	follow

Dear Mr. Fry,

After our telephone conversation, I would like to invite you to the meeting of the Online Encyclopedia Group on November 15th at 7:00 P.M. We will be discussing how to carry forward the proposals for a new interactive website. I have attached a preliminary agenda for the meeting, and also a map showing how to get to the meeting site, 24 Parker Street. A dinner in the evening, to which you are invited, will happen after the meeting.

Let us know if you're coming by November 4th. Can you please bring copies of the sample contract. Feel free to contact us if you have any questions.

Best wishes,

Mary Johnson

Dear Ms. Johnson,

Thank you very much for the invitation to come to the meeting on November 15th, about the plan to start a new website, and thank you also for the agenda. I can come to the meeting.

As asked, I will bring copies of the sample contract. Unfortunately, I won't be able to come to the dinner, because of something I've already organized.

I look forward to seeing you there.

Yours sincerely,

Peter Fry

American English	British English
November 15, 2011	*15 November 2011*

Writing

11a Read the formal email in the Writing Bank on page 76 and do the exercises.

b Read the information in the box and write a formal email. Pay particular attention to greeting and signing off, coherence and cohesion, punctuation, spelling, and style.

You are a celebrity. A Wikipedia entry about you contains some extremely negative comments and a number of factual errors. You tried to edit the Wikipedia entry, but it was "locked," so you were unable to change it. Write a letter of complaint to Wikipedia. Make sure you include corrections of the facts and explain why you think the comments about you are unfair. Ask for the changes to be made as soon as possible.

LESSON 3 **Describe a place** CAN DO

GRAMMAR adjectives

Reading

1 **Pair Work** Discuss. What do you know about the places in the photos? What do you think they are like? Would you like to visit them? Why or why not?

2 Read the descriptions.

Cali

Cali, Colombia

1 In Cali, they say, even the ghosts dance salsa. Its rhythms, born in Cuba, nurtured in New York, and carried on the winds all the way to hot Cali, can be heard in bars, on buses, along the avenues of Juanchito and Plaza Caicedo, and here, too, in a taxi moving at the speed of light, taking me to the heart of the bustling city. The driver slows down at a traffic light, turns to me and says, "*Las calenas* (the women from Cali) are the most beautiful women in the world!" And we're off again, driving past groups of *mulatto* men laughing in the street.

2 My hotel is a run-down old building whose blue paint is peeling in the heat. It has a stunning view from the balcony, and I gaze down on the square. The guidebooks tell you to visit the Gold Museum and the Museum of Colonial Art, the churches of San Antonio and La Merced, but there's only one thing on my mind as I leave the key at reception: salsa dancing.

3 The *salsotecas* don't get busy until midnight, so I stop at a restaurant serving typical Colombian food: *sancocho*—a stew made with chunks of beef, vegetables, cassava (a tropical plant with edible roots), and plantain (a type of banana but not as sweet) served with rice. Then I must choose from the amazingly diverse selection of Colombian fruit. I settle for guanabana and maracuya, and I'm not disappointed. I stroll for a while, tempted by dark smoky cafés, the fans spinning weakly on the ceilings. This is the old, unspoiled Cali, which lives side by side with a newer version, the Cali of junk food, Internet cafés, and vast touristy nightclubs. I walk past the trees and sculptures that line the river and into San Antonio park, a tranquil spot off the beaten track.

4 Later, on Avenida Sexta—Sixth Avenue—I find what I'm really looking for: a *salsoteca*. Some friendly young Colombians teach me a few dance steps, and we chat about Cali. They say that when times are tough, they dance away their worries. By 2:00 A.M. the salsa is swinging, the place is packed, and I know one thing for sure: I've found the Cali that I was looking for—the salsa dancer's paradise.

Koh Chang

Koh Chang, Thailand

5 I had to see this paradise for myself: magnificent stretches of white sandy beaches, dense rainforests, exciting wildlife and marine life, high mountain peaks, and waterfalls. Koh Chang truly is heavenly—a remote, charming, island unspoiled (as yet!) by the modern world.

6 It wasn't easy getting to Koh Chang. My wife and I boarded a rickety overnight bus in Bangkok. We rode for five uncomfortable, sleepless hours to the town of Trat, where we caught an early morning ferry to Center Point Pier in Koh Chang. There we squeezed in the back of a pick-up truck with seven other people and experienced a wild, bumpy ride over the steep winding peaks of the island to our destination: White Sand Beach.

7 And it was truly that—a pure white sand beach. We were engulfed by the tranquility, and our bare feet didn't part with the white sand for three full days. We roasted under the hot sun, gazed at the blue ocean, strolled along the endless beaches, paddled in

canoes along the coastlines, and at night retired to our humble beach hut. We had opted for the simplest of accommodations over the more luxurious villas and resorts that the island also offers.

8 Day four, however, the jungle called, and we ventured away from sun, sand, and sea. A guide walked us through the vast rain forests. We met face-to-face with a tarantula, studied a venomous snake from a distance, and admired a barking deer and a wild pig. I performed a daring high jump into a waterfall that was so clean and refreshing that I then drank from it. My wife was not so brave as to jump, but she did swing on a vine Tarzan-style, waving to the wild monkeys and the exotic birds around us. The guide also showed us a tree used to extract rubber—one of the livelihoods of the inhabitants of Koh Chang. I had no idea rubber comes from trees!

9 The biggest treat was an evening boat tour on our last night. We were met with magical blinking lights on the vast ocean horizon. Our guide informed us these were the boats of local fishermen catching squid. The inhabitants of Koh Chang come from generations of fishermen who still live traditionally, surviving on fishing (as well as growing fruit and rubber). Their ideal balance: go fishing at night and hike or kayak during the day. Sounds like the perfect life to me!

Cape Town

10 The first thing I can tell you about Thabo, my South African guide, is that he is the world's worst driver. From the airport to the heart of the city, he averages 60 miles per hour, swerving around trucks, motorcycles, and taxis crammed with people. The second thing is that he knows everybody and everything about Cape Town. This is good, because I am trying to complete Mission Impossible: see Cape Town in just three days.

11 On the first day, Thabo takes me to the wealthy suburbs with unpronounceable names—Tamboerskloof and Oranjezicht—where you can watch the sun go down on Africa. The views are stunning.

12 The next day we go off the beaten track to Cape Flats, the run-down township where the buildings are made of cardboard and corrugated iron. It is the poorest part of the city and it is vast—nearly a million people live here, side by side. Skinny dogs slide out of the way as Thabo zooms along mud roads lined with trash. Some people wave, others stare. Children run barefoot by the car.

13 Later that night we walk around the bustling Victoria and Alfred Waterfront, Cape Town's most fashionable area. The contrast from the township could not be more stark. As we stroll, the smells of cooking drift up from the kitchens—Asian, French, Italian, and of course South African. The restaurants are packed, and I soon find out why. Cape Town is a paradise for gourmets, seafood-lovers, and people like me, who just like eating. Thabo tells me I can't leave Cape Town without trying some Cape seafood, so I do. It's delicious.

Cape Town, South Africa

14 On my final morning, we spend a tranquil hour sitting outside a café. I gaze at Table Mountain, which forms the backdrop to the city, while Thabo shouts greetings to everyone who passes by. Then we are driving again, experiencing the diverse landscape—sandy beaches, mountain slopes, and green valleys unspoiled by tourism. It's a great way to say goodbye to a place I've known only too briefly. I promise myself, and Thabo, that I'll be back.

3 **Group Work** Discuss.

1. Each place is described as a type of "paradise." Which aspects of these places sound perfect to you? What makes them unique?
2. Which place would you prefer to go to for a vacation? Why?
3. Do you think tourism is good for these three places? What problems might it bring them?

Vocabulary | adjectives to describe places

4 Work in groups. Find words in the article on pages 26–27 that mean:

1. not damaged in character or atmosphere __________ (paragraphs 3, 5, 14)
2. having variety __________ (paragraphs 3, 14)
3. extremely large __________ (paragraphs 3, 8, 9, 12)
4. in poor condition, uncared for __________ (paragraphs 2, 12)
5. amazingly beautiful __________ (paragraphs 2, 11)
6. very busy, crowded __________ (paragraphs 4, 13)
7. peaceful (n. peace) __________, __________ (paragraphs 3, 7, 14)
8. in areas people don't normally go to (usually outside the city) __________ (paragraphs 3, 12)
9. energetic and noisy, full of life __________ (paragraphs 1, 13)
10. extremely impressive and beautiful __________ (paragraph 5)

5 Use the vocabulary in Exercise 4 to complete the sentences.

1. The roof is falling off, and the windows are broken; the old house looks very __________.
2. It's hard to find the little cabin in the countryside because it's __________.
3. You can hardly move during carnival time because the streets are __________.
4. There are many different nationalities living there, so the culture is very __________.
5. The Sahara Desert is 3,630,000 square miles. It's __________.
6. We're going to spend a few __________ days camping, far from the noisy city.
7. The town remains __________, despite the tourists. It hasn't changed at all.
8. The lake is simply __________—it's one of the most beautiful things I've ever seen.

6 **Pair Work** Talk about a place you have been to that a) has stunning views, b) is off the beaten track, c) is tranquil, d) is bustling on the weekends, or e) is unspoiled.

Writing

7a Write a paragraph or two about a favorite place. Think about atmosphere, landscape, things to see and do, and food.

b **Group Work** Exchange paragraphs. Ask questions to learn more about your classmates' favorite places.

How do you get to Silver Beach? What's the best time to go?

Extra Vocabulary Study and Extra Listening Activity in ACTIVEBOOK

Review

1 Complete the sentences, using the gerund or infinitive form of words from the box. You may need to add a preposition.

take	pay	spend	hear	apply	consult	go	buy	live	wear

1. I encouraged the architects ____________ the community about their new project.
2. We didn't mind ____________ a few days in the town, but we didn't want to live there.
3. We urged them not ____________ a house in that area.
4. She's thinking of ____________ for a job as a tour guide.
5. I object ____________ such high rent.
6. They persuaded us ____________ to Koh Chang on our next vacation.
7. I can imagine ____________ here for the rest of my life. I love it.
8. To relieve stress, I recommend ____________ a long vacation once a year.
9. I look forward ____________ from you soon.
10. Members of the ski club are advised ____________ helmets while skiing, for safety.

2 Add one word to complete each sentence.

Ex: Prague is pretty as Vienna.

Prague is as pretty as Vienna.

1. Paraguay is as large as Brazil—Brazil is much larger.
2. Switzerland is the as it always has been: safe, clean and expensive.
3. The more cars we use, the polluted our environment becomes.
4. Poland quite as cold as Norway, but its climate is similar in the northeast.
5. France is a little bit larger Spain.
6. China is far populated than Greenland.
7. Traveling by train is considerably comfortable than traveling by bus.

3 Put the sentences in the correct order. The first two have been done for you.

_1_ Paris is one of the great tourist destinations. Its mild
___ pollution, with a hot air balloon that serves two purposes: it monitors air quality and provides people with stunning
___ of living and have an efficient
___ nightlife, though the crime
___ living is not too high, compared to most of Western Europe. Paris is famous for its cultural
___ healthcare system. Paris has a vibrant
_2_ climate is perfect for relaxing and strolling along the wide streets. Parisians enjoy a good standard
___ life. There are so many wonderful things to do and see. Paris is working to control air
___ views of the city.
___ rate has risen in the last few years. The general cost of

Communication | collaborate on a plan

4a Read the article. Do you think the club is silly, funny, or a good idea?

THE NOT TERRIBLY GOOD CLUB

IN 1976, STEPHEN PILE formed The Not Terribly Good Club. To qualify for membership, you had to do something badly and attend meetings. During these meetings, people gave public demonstrations of things they couldn't do, such as painting or singing, and gave presentations on things they knew nothing about. Stephen Pile kept a record of these unsuccessful events, and then published them as *The Book of Heroic Failures* in 1979. The stories included examples of incompetence, such as "the world's worst tourist," who spent two days in New York, believing he was in Rome; "the slowest completion of a crossword" (34 years); and the burglar who wore metal armor to protect himself from dogs. The armor made so much noise that he got caught, and it was too heavy for him to run away. Included in *The Book of Heroic Failures* was an application form for membership to The Not Terribly Good Club. Amazingly, within two months of the book's publication, the group had received 20,000 applications to join, and the book appeared on various bestseller lists. As a result of his sudden fame, Pile was kicked out of his own club, and the club itself soon disbanded: it had become too successful.

b **Pair Work** If you were joining The Not Terribly Good Club, what would your presentation be about?

5 1.10 Listen to two people describe clubs they belong to. Take notes as you listen. Then compare your notes with a partner.

Alumni club

1. The main purpose of the club
2. Other things that members do
3. Type of meeting
4. Who can be a member

Ballroom dancing club

1. Number of people in the club
2. When and where it meets
3. Things members have learned

6a **Group Work** Imagine that you are going to form a club. Think about the following questions.

1. What type of club is it?
2. What events will you organize?
3. What are the goals of the club?
4. What is the name of the club?
5. Where will you meet?
6. How often?
7. What rules will the club have?

b Present your ideas to the rest of the class. Which clubs would you like to join?

UNIT 3
Stories

Warm Up

1 **Pair Work** Discuss. Can you identify any of the stories illustrated by the pictures? What types of stories do they illustrate?

2 Think of an example for each of the story types listed below. Use your dictionary if necessary.

1. a fake 2. a myth 3. a tall tale 4. a fairy tale 5. a legend 6. a joke

3 **Pair Work** Discuss the meanings of the phrases in bold. Then answer the questions.

1. Do you think it's OK to **tell a white lie** if it makes life easier?
2. Have you ever taken part in (or heard about) **a hoax**?
3. When you describe things, do you sometimes **exaggerate**?
4. Do you know any **good storytellers**?
5. Were you told **bedtime stories** when you were a child? Which were your favorites?

Tell an anecdote

GRAMMAR review of past forms

CAN DO

Reading

1 **Pair Work** Look at the photos and discuss the questions.

1. What can you tell about Manuel Elizalde from the photo?
2. Who do you think Sidd Finch was?

2 Read the article. Then answer the questions that follow.

HOAXES THAT FOOLED THE WORLD

Manuel Elizalde and the Tasaday people

In 1971, while he was working as a government minister in the Philippines, Manuel Elizalde announced a great discovery. He had found a Stone Age tribe, the Tasaday, living in a remote part of the country. They lived in caves, used stone tools, and ate any food they could find. This isolated tribe, just 27 people, had been living this way for many generations. Journalists arrived from all over the world, a documentary about the tribe was filmed for TV, and thousands of dollars were spent on research trips. The Philippine government, however, not wanting to destroy a way of life that had existed for thousands of years, allowed only a few people to visit them.

It was only years later that the truth came out. Researchers found the tribe living in villages, wearing Levi's jeans and communicating happily with other people. They explained that they had been pretending all along; Elizalde had paid them to act like a Stone Age tribe.

Elizalde's hoax was just one in a long line. Anthropology has been a particularly rich field for hoaxers, including Fujimura Shinichi, the Japanese archaeologist who faked vital discoveries for years before being found out in 2000.

But perhaps the most interesting hoaxes are those that involve fictitious people. Piotr Zak was, as reported by the BBC, a Polish composer. An avant-garde modernist, he was not well-known among the public. At least not until 1961, when the BBC broadcast his piece *Mobile for Tape and Percussion*. Some music critics hailed it as a great work. Unfortunately for them, the piece had consisted of BBC staff making strange noises, edited by BBC technicians. It was a classic hoax.

Nearly a quarter of a century later, on April 1, 1985, another great hoax was to shake the world of American sports. In the United States, April 1 is April Fools' Day, a day for playing practical jokes. *Sports Illustrated* ran an article about Sidd Finch, a truly extraordinary baseball player. The subheading of the article read: "He's a pitcher, part yogi and part recluse. Impressively liberated from our opulent lifestyle, Sidd's deciding about yoga—and his future in baseball." Read the first letters of these words again, carefully. They spell out "Happy April Fools' Day." On April 15, the magazine came clean: They had fooled their readers. Finch was an invention. The writer of the article, George Plimpton, then extended his article into a novel, published in 1987.

Just a year later, British writer William Boyd published *Nat Tate: American Artist, 1928–1960*, the tragic biography of a New York painter. A number of prominent critics claimed to remember Tate's work, claiming that he had been one of the greatest artists of the century. He'd never existed. The name Nat Tate is derived from two of Britain's most famous art galleries: The National Gallery (Nat) and the Tate Gallery.

Sidd Finch

1. Why do you think people were so excited about the discovery of the Tasaday tribe?
2. Why do you think the people in the reading created these hoaxes?
3. Why do you think that intelligent people such as journalists and academics fall for hoaxes?

Grammar | review of past forms

3a Read the first paragraph of the article in Exercise 2 again. Find examples of the simple past, past continuous, past perfect, and past perfect continuous.

b Look at the pairs of sentences below. What are the differences in meaning (if any)?

1. a. When the truth came out, Elizalde had already left the country.
   b. When the truth came out, Elizalde left the country.
2. a. People believed the tribe had been living the same way for centuries.
   b. People believed the tribe had lived the same way for centuries.
3. a. When researchers arrived, the people from the tribe weren't living in caves any more.
   b. When researchers arrived, the people from the tribe didn't live in caves any more.

4 Complete the rules in the Active Grammar box with words from the box.

progress	length
chronological	before

Active Grammar

1. Use the simple past for past finished actions. Use it to describe a sequence of events in ___________ order.
2. Use the past continuous for actions in ___________ when something else happened.
3. Use the past perfect for actions completed ___________ other events in the past. Use it when you are already talking about the past.
4. Use the past perfect continuous for actions already in progress before the main events happened. Use it to emphasize the ___________ of the action.

See Reference page 69

5a Complete the descriptions of some famous hoaxes with the correct form of the verbs in parentheses.

1 In 1957 a news program called *Panorama* broadcast a story about spaghetti trees in Switzerland. While the reporter told the story, Swiss farmers in the background ___________ (1. pick) spaghetti from trees. Following this, thousands of people ___________ (2. call) the show, asking how to grow spaghetti trees.

2 In 1998 large numbers of Americans went to Burger King asking for a new type of burger. The food company ___________ (3. publish) an ad in *USA Today* announcing the new "left-handed Whopper," a burger designed for left-handed people. The following day, Burger King ___________ (4. admit) that they ___________ (5. joke) all along.

b 1.11 Listen and check your answers.

Speaking

6a Prepare to tell a story about something that has happened in your life. Include in your story two or three details that are *not* true. Think about the following:

1. What were you doing when it happened?
2. Where were you? Who were you with?
3. What had happened before this?
4. What happened next?

b **Pair Work** Tell your story. Try to guess which details in your partner's story are invented.

It was the summer of 2009. I had been hanging out at the pool with my friends all morning, when suddenly . . .

Vocabulary | synonyms

7a Read the newspaper excerpts. Think of synonyms for the underlined words and phrases.

1 The president is under pressure to combat illegal immigration after another state took drastic measures to deal with the problem yesterday.

2 Two men have been detained by police in connection with a bank robbery. The police stopped a truck loaded with cars that may have been purchased by the thieves.

3 In order to keep track of cows, which are considered sacred in India, authorities in Delhi are placing microchips in the animals.

4 The government has initiated a series of talks to settle the dispute that led to chaos on the trains.

5 A PROMINENT doctor claims that the country's failure to prevent the yearly outbreak of flu arises from a lack of hygiene in schools.

b Match the words to the underlined words and phrases with similar meanings in Exercise 7a.

1. stop ____________
2. fight ____________
3. resolve ____________
4. follow the movements ____________
5. extreme actions ____________
6. asserts ____________
7. arrested ____________
8. stems ____________
9. packed ____________
10. putting ____________
11. thought to be ____________
12. formal discussions ____________
13. cope with ____________
14. caused ____________
15. bought ____________
16. started ____________

8 **Pair Work** Complete the crossword puzzle. All of the words are from the article on page 32.

Across

1. faking (v)
2. alone (adj)
4. extremely important (adj)
5. freed (adj)
7. ruin (v)
10. tricked (v)

Down

1. well-known and usually well-respected (adj)
3. imagined/invented (adj)
6. expanded (v)
8. extremely sad (adj)
9. a big, elaborate trick (n)

LESSON 2 Describe a person in detail

CAN DO

GRAMMAR compound adjectives

Vocabulary | books

1 **Pair Work** Discuss.

1. What kind of books do you like reading?
2. What are your three favorite books?

2 Match the sentences with similar meanings.

____ 1. I couldn't put it down.
____ 2. It's very readable.
____ 3. It's a page-turner.
____ 4. I found the story very moving.
____ 5. The characters are one-dimensional.
____ 6. It's based on a true story.
____ 7. I'm a real bookworm.
____ 8. It's a best-seller.

a. I'm an avid reader.
b. I was hooked.
c. It was gripping.
d. It depicts real events.
e. It has a nice, easy style.
f. It has sold many copies.
g. I was emotionally involved in it.
h. They didn't really come alive for me.

3 **Group Work** Think of different books that could be described by the words in Exercise 2. Tell other students about them.

The Road Home *isn't a best-seller, but I thought it was a wonderful story. I couldn't put it down.*

Listening

4a 1.12 Listen to three people answering some of the questions below. Complete the chart.

	Speaker 1	Speaker 2	Speaker 3
1. Who is your favorite fictional character?			
2. Why do you like or admire this character?			
3. What do you think the character looks like?			
4. What personal traits does he or she possess (type of character)?			
5. What problems does he or she overcome?			

b Listen again to check your answers.

5 **Pair Work** Who is your favorite fictional character? Spend a few minutes thinking about your own answers to the questions in Exercise 4a. Then discuss.

Reading

6 Read the book excerpts and answer the questions. There may be more than one possible answer.

1. Which excerpt describes a dangerous character?
2. Which excerpt describes a middle-aged and not very handsome character?
3. Which excerpt describes a character who is probably bossy?
4. Which excerpt describes a character who probably spends a lot of time outdoors?
5. Which excerpt describes a character who is old but has a young mind?

1

For one thing, he was unlike any other man we'd ever seen—or heard of, if it came to that. With his **weather-beaten** face, wide teeth-crammed mouth, and **far-seeing** blue eyes, he looked like some wigwam warrior stained with suns and heroic slaughter.

(*The Edge of Day*—Laurie Lee)

2

My father is still living, but less and less. Judge James Charles Endicott Jackson . . . that tall, lean, **hollow-cheeked** man who had made such a religion of the law, preached from the head of our dining-room table each evening of my young life.

(*The Best Revenge*—Sol Stein)

3

He was fifty-five, but he could have been ten years either side of that. Thin sandy hair, a big awkward mouth. Bad teeth, crooked and dark when he smiled, jug-handle ears. As a **self-conscious** boy he'd tried different things with those ears. He'd made an elasticized band with elaborate leather flaps to flatten his ears while he slept. He'd tried his hair short. He'd tried it long. He'd tried all kinds of hats. Eventually he'd grown the moustache as a kind of diversionary tactic, and he'd kept it.

(*The Idea of Perfection*—Kate Grenville)

4

Her grandmother was small and thin, with tiny hands and feet—**fast-moving** feet the size of a child's—and **washed-out** red frizzy hair that she dyed the color of Red Delicious apples. She had disappearing lips, painted large, twice their size, the color of plums. All her life, she'd been a dancer, every kind of dancer. Even now, at seventy-seven, she'd put on tights and a leotard and tutu, and do her ballet exercises in front of the long mirror on Alyssa's bedroom door.

(*Blister*—Susan Shreve)

5

He was just a **hot-headed**, twenty-year-old kid at the time, but he was greasy-fast with a gun. The problem was that he was spoiling for a fight and got it. At over six feet and one hundred and ninety pounds, he was a big boy and he had set out to prove to everyone that he was a man to reckon with.

(*Slade*—Robert Dyer)

7 **Group Work** Read the excerpts again and answer the questions.

1. What type of person is being described in each excerpt?
2. What physical details are included? Do they show the person's character?
3. What actions are shown? How do these reveal character?
4. What type of book do you think each excerpt is from (funny, serious, etc.)?
5. Would you like to read any of the books?

Grammar | compound adjectives

8 Read the Active Grammar box and answer the questions after each rule.

Active Grammar

1. We often use compound adjectives, such as *kind-hearted*, to describe people. Which compound adjectives in the book excerpts on page 36
   a) describe someone's character?
   b) describe something physical?
2. Compound adjectives frequently use a hyphen (-) between the words. Often the second word is a present or past participle.
3. Sometimes we can guess the meaning of compound adjectives. What is the compound adjective for a person who works hard? keeps an open mind? looks good? thinks freely? loves fun?

See Reference page 69

9 **Pair Work** Read the sentences. Try to explain in your own words what the compound adjectives in bold mean.

1. He's very **single-minded**. It took him ten years to learn the violin, but he never gave up!
2. She's very **self-sufficient** for a child. She makes her own food and entertains herself for hours.
3. Writers have to be **thick-skinned**. Lots of people criticize their work, but they try not to get upset.
4. He's so **kind-hearted**. He's always helpful, even if he's busy.
5. They can be a little **stand-offish**. They didn't talk to anybody at the party.
6. He's very **career-oriented**. He even brings work on vacation.
7. They're really **level-headed**. Even when they won all that money, they didn't get too excited.
8. I'm a little bit **absent-minded**. I keep forgetting where I put my glasses.

Writing

10a Read the How To box and write a short description of someone you know well. Describe the following: first impressions, physical details, and character. Use at least two compound adjectives.

How To:

Describe people

First impressions	• *She **comes across as** (adjective), but **once you get to know** her, she's (adjective).* • ***The thing that strikes you about** him is that . . .*
Character—good things and bad things	• ***The thing I (don't) like about** her is . . .* • ***What I (don't) really like about** him is . . .* • *She's **so** (adjective)* • *He's **such a** (adjective) person* • *She **can be a bit** (negative adjective)*

b **Group Work** Share your descriptions. Ask questions.

Paul seems shy at first, but once you get to know him, he's very friendly.

What makes him appear shy?

LESSON 3

Tell a joke

GRAMMAR phrases with participles and gerunds

CAN DO

Reading

1 **Pair Work** Who are your favorite comedians? What makes them funny?

2 Read about Groucho Marx. Guess the answer to the question at the end of each section.

King of the Jokers

1 Julius Henry Marx was born in New York on October 2, 1890. His father was a tailor and his mother, Minnie, was a promoter for her brother, comedian Al Shean. Growing up with a comedian in the family would be important later. But, as a child, Groucho's first love was reading. He was also an extremely good singer.

What happened next?

a. *He became a singer.*
b. *He wrote a book.*
c. *He started performing with his uncle.*

Go to 4 to find out. →

2 Groucho became host of a radio show called *You Bet Your Life.* It was so popular that they moved it to TV. Groucho would interview the contestants and ad-lib jokes. Some of the more memorable questions included: "What color is the White House?" and "Who is buried in Grant's Tomb?" Returned now to national prominence, Groucho embarked on his solo film career, with a string of films throughout the '50s and '60s. But by now he was entering his 70s.

What happened next?

a. *Groucho went to live in the Bahamas, for health reasons.*
b. *Groucho started writing fiction.*
c. *Groucho returned to fame in the 1970s.*

Go to 8 to find out. →

3 Desperately attempting to win some money, Groucho met Irving Thalberg, a big name in Hollywood, during a card game. Thalberg, impressed with his new friend's act, helped the Marx Brothers to get established in the movie business. In the 1930s, the brothers made their most famous movies: *A Night at the Opera* (1935) and *A Day at the Races* (1937).

What happened next?

a. *Groucho got sick and then retired.*
b. *The Marx Brothers disbanded.*
c. *The brothers set up their own production company, which made them rich.*

Go to 5 to find out. →

4 At the age of 14, he began singing with the LeRoy Trio. His first tour wasn't a great experience—the trio abandoned him in Colorado. Having been left behind, Groucho had to work his way back home. At this stage he wanted to become a doctor, but his mother had other plans for him.

What happened next?

a. *He ran away to study medicine.*
b. *Groucho and his brothers formed a musical act.*
c. *Groucho won a TV competition.*

Go to 7 to find out. →

5 Following a movie called *The Big Store* (1941), the Marx Brothers disbanded. It seemed as though Groucho was going to fade into obscurity, when suddenly another opportunity arose.

What happened?

a. *He started a radio show.*
b. *He became a politician.*
c. *He went to medical school.*

Go to 2 to find out. →

6 After suffering a severe stroke, Minnie died. Then the stock market crashed, signaling the beginning of the Great Depression. After hitting the heights of fame and fortune, suddenly Groucho and his brothers lost everything. Depressed by the situation, Groucho began to suffer from insomnia.

How did the Marx Brothers recover in the 1930s?

a. *They invested in property.*
b. *They toured the world, playing in small theaters.*
c. *They started making movies.*

Go to 3 to find out. →

7 Groucho and his brothers, encouraged by their ambitious mother, formed a group called The Six Mascots, which lasted only a short time. Having been no more than a moderate success, one day they suddenly started cracking jokes on stage. The audience loved it. Being funny came naturally to them. Soon the Marx Brothers were performing all over the country. Groucho, with his fast-talking characters, chicken-walk, painted-on mustache, big glasses, and a cigar that he never smoked, was the star. Then everything changed in 1929.

What happened in 1929?

a. *The brothers' mother died and Groucho lost all his money.*
b. *Groucho went to live on a Pacific island.*
c. *The brothers argued about money and split up their act.*

Go to 6 to find out. →

8 Groucho made a comeback in the 1970s with a live one-man show. But with his health failing, he retired. He died of pneumonia in 1977, at the age of 86. Voted the fifth greatest comedy act ever by his fellow comedians in a 2005 poll, Groucho lives on, at least in memory. Everyone recognizes those famous glasses with the fake nose and mustache.

THE END

3 ▶1.13 **Pair Work** Listen to someone describing Groucho Marx's life. Find the speaker's mistakes.

They didn't start telling jokes during a radio show. They started . . .

Grammar | phrases with participles and gerunds

4 Complete the task after each rule in the Active Grammar box.

Active Grammar

Exercise 2 contains several examples of participles and gerunds.

There are two types of participle: past participles (*-ed* forms for regular verbs) and present participles (*-ing* forms).

A gerund is a verb + *-ing* that functions as a noun.

1. We often use participles to add extra information to the idea in the sentence. The past participle sometimes acts as an adjective. The present participle sometimes gives background information.

   ***Returned** now to national prominence, Groucho embarked on his solo film career . . .* (section 2)

   Find an example with a past participle and one with a present participle in section 3.

   ____

   ____

2. *Having* + past participle shows the cause of a second action (or a sequence of actions).

   ***Having been** left behind, Groucho had to work his way back home.* (section 4)

   Find another example in section 7.

   ____

3. We often use a present participle after conjunctions (*after, before, when*).

   ***After suffering** a severe stroke, Minnie died.* (section 6)

   Find another example in section 6.

   ____

4. We can use a gerund as the subject of the sentence.

   ***Being funny** came naturally to them.* (section 7)

   Find another example in section 1.

   ____

See Reference page 69

5 Complete the sentences, using a participle or gerund of the verb in the parentheses.

1. When __________ (tell) a joke, timing is very important.
2. __________ (work) as a comedian must be a great job, because you make people laugh.
3. __________ (make) to look out of date by modern comics, comedians from the past aren't fully appreciated.
4. __________ (tell) jokes in a foreign language is extremely difficult.
5. On __________ (be) told a joke, you should laugh even if you don't think it's funny.
6. After __________ (watch) Chaplin, I think physical humor can be very funny.

6 **Pair Work** Do you agree with the statements in Exercise 5? Compare your views.

Vocabulary | humor

7 Match the types of humor to the correct definitions. Use your dictionary to check any words you don't understand.

___ 1. bizarre (very strange) humor	a. farce
___ 2. light, humorous play or movie with an unrealistic plot and exaggerated characters	b. puns
___ 3. humor conveyed by pictures or animation	c. cartoons
___ 4. jokes about death and other serious issues	d. black humor
___ 5. word play	e. surreal humor
___ 6. not saying exactly what you mean, or saying the opposite of what you mean	f. irony
___ 7. saying something is much more than it is	g. exaggeration
___ 8. laughing at politicians and famous people	h. satire

8 **Pair Work** Discuss.

1. Do you know any famous actors, comedians, writers, or movies associated with the types of humor from Exercise 7?
2. Which types of humor do you like best?

Listening

9a ▶1.14 Cover the reading below and listen to a joke. Do you think it is funny?

b Why do you think the speaker pauses at certain moments? Listen again and read the joke. Mark the pauses. The first one has been done for you.

Three colleagues, a photographer, a journalist and an editor are covering a political convention. | One day, during their lunch break, they walk along a beach and one of them sees a lamp. He picks it up and rubs it, and a magic genie suddenly appears. The genie says, "You can each have one wish." So the photographer says, "I want to spend the rest of my life in a big house in the mountains with a beautiful view, where I can take photographs." Poof! Suddenly the photographer is gone to his home in the mountains. Then it's the journalist's turn. "I want to live in a big house in the countryside with an enormous garden where I can sit and write for the rest of my life." Poof! The journalist is gone. Finally, the genie says to the editor, "And what about you? What's your wish?" So the editor says, "I want those two back before lunch. We've got a deadline at 6:00 tonight."

Speaking

10a **SPEAKING EXCHANGE** Work in groups of three. You are going to tell a joke. Student A: turn to page 74. Student B: turn to page 73. Student C: turn to page 75. Read your joke two or three times and try to memorize it.

b Tell the joke to the other students in your group. Whose joke was the funniest? Who told it best?

Review

1 Circle the correct choices to complete the paragraph.

In April 2000, journalists at *Esquire* magazine (**1.** *decided/were deciding*) that life at the magazine was getting a little bit boring. So they published an article about FreeWheelz, an Internet company that gave customers free cars covered in advertising. The article (**2.** *had claimed/claimed*) that FreeWheelz "will transform the auto industry more than Henry Ford did." The company (**3.** *hadn't/didn't*) yet become famous but it would "on April 1, when FreeWheelz launches on the web for real." Readers who (**4.** *were seeing/saw*) the website, which had been created by the author of the article, were impressed. Within days, the site had (**5.** *received/been receiving*) over a thousand hits and messages from other entrepreneurs who claimed that they had been planning similar businesses. The website contained a questionnaire for potential clients that (**6.** *included/was including*) strange questions such as "Does hair loss concern you?" In the next edition, the magazine owned up, explaining that the article had been an April Fools' hoax. The magazine (**7.** *had forgotten/forgot*) all about it when suddenly an offer for the domain name FreeWheelz came in. The author of the article sold the name for $25,000, splitting the profits with the owners of the magazine. The conclusion? Never trust a strange story containing the date April 1.

2 Rewrite the sentences without changing the meaning. Use participial phrases or gerunds. Use the verb in parentheses.

Ex: Because we couldn't find our way, we had to turn back. (lose)
Lost, we had to turn back.

Robbie ate all the cherries, and then he was sick. (have/eat)
Having eaten all the cherries, Robbie was sick.

1. Life's biggest pleasure is when you do things for other people. (do)
2. Anyone who wishes to take the exam must register in June. (wish)
3. Most of the jewelry that thieves stole from the store has been recovered by the police. (steal)
4. Because she felt sleepy, Luisa went to bed. (feel)
5. When you swim, you must wear a bathing cap. (swim)
6. He had been famous for years, and he finally wanted some peace and quiet. (have/be)
7. Because they were censored in their own country, they decided to publish their book overseas. (censor)
8. David woke up early and went for a run. (wake up)

3 Put the letters in parentheses in the correct order to complete the web posts.

Posted by Nico

I am a complete *bookworm* (**Ex:** bmrooowk), and I'm an ________ (**1.** ivda) reader of Spike Davies's fiction. His latest book, *Charms*, is a real ________ (**2.** eapg-eutnrr). It's full of ________ (**3.** albkc uhrom), which made me laugh aloud. I was absolutely ________ (**4.** odehko).

[posted 04:41 PM, viewed 10 times]

Posted by Nina J

I'd say that *Charms* is very ________ (**5.** rbadlaee), but I thought that the characters were a bit ________ (**6.** oen-idsilanomne) compared to his other books. His previous book, which was ________ (**7.** edbsa) on a true story, was very ________ (**8.** ggniprpi)—in fact I ________ (**9.** ulcdno't tup ti dnow). I wasn't surprised it became a ________ (**10.** sebt-lelres). But *Charms* has too many weak ________ (**11.** sunp), and it lacks the clever ________ (**12.** ynior) of his best work.

[posted 05:22 PM, viewed 8 times]

Communication | tell a story

4a **Group Work** Read the opening sentences to some pieces of fiction and discuss the questions.

1. Is there anything unusual about the situation described?
2. Where and when do you think each book is set? What makes you think this?
3. What can you guess about each story? What type of story might it be?
4. Which excerpts make you want to read more? Why?

b Choose one of the story openings and discuss how the story could continue. Decide who will tell each part of the story, and practice telling it together.

. . . Parker kicked the door in. Inside, he found a man sitting in a . . .

c Tell your story to another group. Which group has the most interesting or unusual story?

1. Milena boiled things. She was frightened of disease. She would boil other people's knives and forks before using them.
(*The Child Garden*—Geoff Ryman)

2. I'm often asked what it's like to be married to a genius. The question used to please me . . .
(*The Mind-Body Problem*—Rebecca Goldstein)

3. It was a bright cold day in April, and the clocks were striking thirteen.
(*1984*—George Orwell)

4. If I am out of my mind, it's all right with me, thought Moses Herzog.
(*Herzog*—Saul Bellow)

5. Rose Pickles knew something bad was going to happen. Something really bad this time.
(*Cloudstreet*—Tim Winton)

6. When he didn't get any answer the second time he knocked, Parker kicked the door in.
(*The Split*—Richard Stark)

7. As Gregor Samsa awoke one morning from uneasy dreams, he found himself transformed in his bed into a gigantic insect.
(*Metamorphosis*—Franz Kafka)

8. All children, except one, grow up.
(*Peter Pan*—J.M. Barrie)

9. It was a wrong number that started it, the telephone ringing three times in the dead of night, and the voice on the other end asking for someone he was not.
(*The New York Trilogy*—Paul Auster)

UNIT 4
Moving forward

A

B

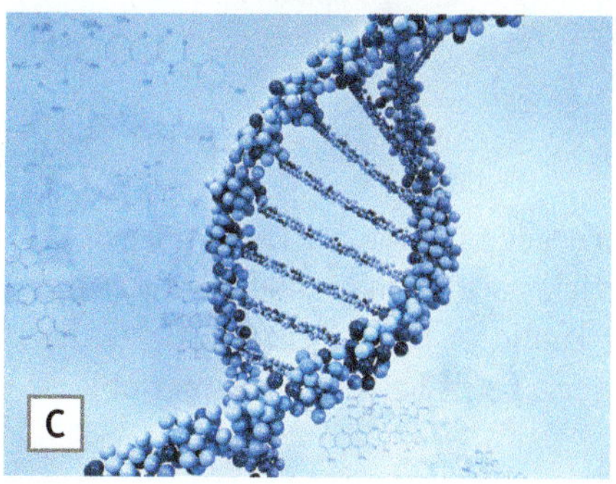

C

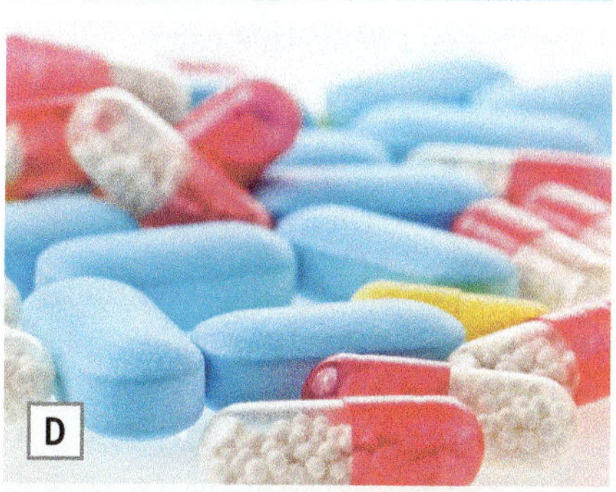

D

Warm Up

1 **Pair Work** Discuss. What types of progress are shown in the photos? What developments have there been recently? What developments might there be in the future?

2a Match the news headlines to the photos.

____ 1. Resistance to antibiotics on the increase
____ 2. New virus destroys global computer systems
____ 3. Genetic engineering breakthrough provides hope for many
____ 4. Space mission in danger as budget crisis grows

b ▶ 1.15 Listen to the news stories.

3 **Pair Work** Check the meaning of the words in bold and then answer the questions.

1. Would you describe yourself as a "**computer nerd**" or a "**technophobe**"?
2. Are you **up-to-date** with the **latest technology**? Are there any new **gadgets** that you would like to buy?
3. Do you enjoy reading scientific **journals** or watching **documentaries**? Which scientific areas interest you most? Why?

Describe the chances of something happening

GRAMMAR future probability

Speaking

1 **Pair Work** Discuss. Do you (or did you ever) enjoy movies or comic books featuring superheroes? Who are your favorite characters?

2a **Group Work** You have four minutes to test your knowledge of superheroes. Write down:

1. the names of four different superheroes
2. the color of the Incredible Hulk
3. four of Spider Man's five special powers
4. the name of the planet where Superman was born
5. the name of the superhero movie released in 2002 that broke all box-office records on its very first weekend
6. the name of the female character who has super-strength, bullet-proof bracelets, and a lasso that makes people tell the truth

b 1.16 Listen and check your answers.

Reading

3 Read the article about research into real-life super powers.

HOW TO BE A SUPERHERO

Got what it takes to become a superhero? For most of us the answer is a resounding *no*. But that hasn't stopped scientists from trying to recreate super powers artificially. And you might be surprised at how successful they have been.

Wall climbing

Gecko lizards are so good at this that they can hang upside down from a glass surface by a single toe. The secret lies in the millions of tiny hairs, called *setae*, which are on the gecko's skin. Now scientists at Manchester University are developing a material covered with similar nanoscopic hairs that would enable a person to walk on a ceiling or up a wall. One square centimeter of the tape holds 100 million artificial setae and could support a kilogram of weight. There is a fairly good chance that this system could allow people to walk up walls.

Teleportation

Just as superhero Nightcrawler can teleport, scientists in Australia have discovered how to teleport matter for real—albeit on the atomic scale, for the time being. The researchers have succeeded in transmitting information about quantum particles across space and then using it to reassemble exact copies of the original particles. It is unlikely that the process will be used for larger objects.

Regeneration

Both Superman and the X-men's Wolverine can regenerate tissue instantly—they can be hit by a bullet and recover in seconds. Doctors at a children's hospital in Boston have pioneered a similar way of helping terminally ill patients to re-grow healthy organs. There is every likelihood that the procedure could eventually be commonly used to grow organs for transplants.

Super-strength

No matter how many steroids you take, you don't stand a chance of achieving the strength of the Incredible Hulk. However, there is a distinct possibility that genetics could help those seeking a Hulk-like physique. Johns Hopkins University scientists have created Mighty Mouse—a rodent that has been genetically modified so that a protein that limits muscle-growth is blocked. "They are normal in every respect, except their muscles are two to three times larger than normal," says molecular biologist Se Jin-Lee. "They look like Schwarzenegger mice." Presumably, it will also help scientists to better understand muscle-wasting diseases.

Force field

Superman's hideaway, the Fortress of Solitude, is protected by a force field. The Defense Science and Technology Laboratory run by the UK Ministry of Defense has developed a similar force field to protect tanks from rocket-propelled grenades. Once shielded by the force field, there is very little chance that the tanks can be destroyed.

Web-shooter

The US army has developed a device for the New York police that acts like Spider Man's webshooter. The nets are designed to restrain people without causing serious injury and are shot from a kind of stun gun. The victim caught in the net stands no chance of escape, as the nets come in three varieties: a regular net, one that can give an electric shock, and—most fittingly of all, one that becomes sticky on contact with air. These crime-stopping devices are bound to cause some sticky problems for New York criminals!

X-ray vision

Everyone would love to have Superman's ability to see through walls. But the odds are against the general use of X-rays, as they are dangerous, and repeated exposure to them isn't good for your health. The solution could be "terahertz imaging." Terahertz radiation lies between the infrared and microwave regions of the spectrum, so these low-energy rays can penetrate matter just like X-rays but without the harmful effects. Researchers are developing them for defense and medical imaging.

Flying

Superman has the ability to fly without the aid of wings or rockets. Researchers have looked into the possibility of using spinning discs to defy gravity. The original research was carried out by a Russian researcher working in Finland in 1996, but so far no other researchers have managed to verify his claim. It is doubtful that we will be able to achieve this in the foreseeable future.

Invisibility

The Invisible Woman is part of the Fantastic Four. Now a virtual reality expert in Japan has created a "see-through" coat, which appears to make the wearer's body disappear. The material is coated with microscopic reflectors that work like a movie screen. A tiny video camera is then attached to the back of the coat. The image from the back of the coat is projected onto the front of the coat, which makes observers think that they can see through it.

4 **Group Work** Discuss. Which research described in the article do you think is important? Which do you think is less important? Does any of the research worry you?

Actually, the research into terahertz imaging worries me a little bit. What if . . .

Grammar | future probability

5 Complete the task and fill in the chart in the Active Grammar box.

Active Grammar

To talk about future probability, we can use modal verbs *will*, *could*, *may*, and *might*.

We can also use phrases such as those in the chart. Which phrases are used to talk about future probability in the article on pages 44–45? Underline them and then add them to the chart.

1. Will almost definitely happen	• *It will presumably . . .*
2. Likely to happen	• *The chances are that . . .* • *There is a strong possibility . . .* • *It may/might well . . .*
3. Unlikely to happen	• *There's a slight/remote possibility that . . .* • *I doubt whether . . .* • *It probably won't . . .* • *The chances are slim that . . .*
4. Impossible	• *It is inconceivable that . . .*

See Reference page 70

6 Rewrite the sentences, using the words in parentheses, keeping the meaning the same.

Ex: There is no chance that she's borrowing my laptop. (stand)
She doesn't stand a chance of borrowing my laptop.

1. It's highly unlikely that they will make a breakthrough in the near future. (doubtful)
2. It isn't possible that we'll be able to travel to Mars by 2050. (inconceivable)
3. I'm sure they'll notice it's missing. (bound)
4. We can't be entirely confident that the information is secure. (chance)
5. We're being met at the airport, so we don't need train tickets. (presumably)
6. China has a good chance of winning the space race. (distinct)
7. There doesn't seem to be much hope that the relationship will improve. (doubt)

Speaking

7 **Pair Work** Discuss. What are the chances of the following happening in the next 20 years?

1. We will be able to go on vacation in space.
2. There will be a cure for cancer or AIDS.
3. Nuclear energy will have been abolished.
4. Parents will be able to choose the gender, hair color, and eye color of their babies.
5. All foods will be genetically modified.

Listening

8 ▶ 1.17 Listen to an interview with Stan Lee, the creator of Spider Man. In what order does he answer the questions below? What are his answers?

____ a. Will there ever be real superheroes?
____ b. Why did he make Spider Man a scientist?
____ c. How did you think of Spider Man?
____ d. Are you at all scientific?

LESSON 2 Talk about plans and arrangements

CAN DO

GRAMMAR future forms: review

Vocabulary | arrangements

1 **Pair Work** Discuss.

1. How do you keep in touch with your family and friends?
2. Read the quotation.

   "Modern communications technology is designed to keep us too busy to actually see anyone."
   (*Paul Mendez, psychologist*)

   Do you agree with Mendez? Do you think communications technology has made our lives better or worse?

2a Read the emails below. What is Tom trying to do? What happens in the end?

1

Hi, Mel and Alec—
What **are** you **up to** this Sunday? If you're **free**, come over to my place. We're going to have a barbecue.
Tom

2

Hi, Tom—
Thanks for the offer, but I'm completely **swamped** right now. I have to write an essay by Monday afternoon, so I'll be working all weekend. I don't have anything **lined up** for next weekend though, so maybe we can get together then? I'll call you later.
Alec

3

Dear Tom,
I'm **tied up** tomorrow, too. I'm going to my great uncle's house for a family lunch. He wasn't feeling well, so we thought it might **fall through**, but it looks like **it's on**. I really can't **get out of** it, because it's his 60th birthday, and most of my family will probably be there. Sorry!
Mel

4

OK you guys,
I'm **calling off** the barbecue. According to the weather forecast, it's going to rain all weekend anyway.
Maybe you'll have finished what you have to do by 9:00 or so, and we can go out instead! If you want to **wind down**, I'll be at Paola's, a restaurant on King Street. Gloria and I are meeting there at about 8:30, as long as nothing else **comes up**! Don't forget it closes at 11 on Sundays.
Talk to you soon,
Tom

b Read the emails again and match the words or phrases in bold to the definitions below.

1. ____________: be engaged in activity
2. ____________: arrive unexpectedly
3. ____________: busy/not free
4. ____________: planned/arranged
5. ____________: avoid doing something
6. ____________: cancel
7. ____________: extremely busy
8. ____________: not happen or take place (a plan)
9. ____________: proceed as expected (a plan)
10. ____________: have no plans/available
11. ____________: become relaxed

3 Add the missing word to each sentence.

1. The tennis match was called due to rain.
2. If you aren't to anything this afternoon, why don't you come over?
3. I'm sorry—I won't be able to make it at 5:30. Something has come.
4. I'm tied all of January, but I'll have some free time in February.
5. There's a great new band lined for tonight.
6. I need to wind after this lousy week.
7. Despite the rain, the festival is still.
8. She can't come tomorrow, because she's with work.
9. I have to clean the house today. I can't get out it.
10. The picnic plans fell when the forecast called for rain.

Grammar | future forms: review

4 Read the emails in Exercise 2a again. Which verb forms are used for talking about the future? Complete the tasks in the Active Grammar box.

Active Grammar

Complete each rule with the correct ending.

1. Use the **simple present** __e__
   *Don't forget it **closes** at 11 on Sundays.*
2. Use **will** ______
   ***I'll call** you later.*
3. Use **will** ______
   *Most of my family **will probably be** there.*
4. Use **be going to** or the present continuous ______
   ***We're going to have** a barbecue.*
   *Gloria and I **are meeting** there at about 8:30.*
5. Use **be going to** ______
   *According to the weather forecast, **it's going to rain** anyway.*
6. Use the **future continuous** ______
   ***I'll be working** all weekend.*
7. Use the **future perfect** ______
   *Maybe **you'll have finished** what you have to do by 9:00 or so.*

a. for predictions you make because of present evidence.
b. for something that will be finished before a time in the future.
c. for immediate decisions made at the same time as you speak or write.
d. for something you think, guess or calculate about the future.
e. for fixed timetables, schedules, and arrangements.
f. for something that will be in progress during a period of time in the future.
g. for a personal intention or for fixed plans or arrangements.

See Reference page 70

5a Make questions, using *will*, the future continuous, or the future perfect.

In one year:

1. Do you think you ______________ (still study) English?
2. Do you think you ______________ (have) the same lifestyle?
3. Do you think you ______________ (live) in the same place?
4. Do you think your country ______________ (have) a different government?

In ten years:

5. Do you think you ______________ (change) much?
6. Do you think you ______________ (have) the same interests?
7. Do you think you ______________ (have) the same close friends?
8. Do you think you ______________ (see) more of the world?

b 1.18 Listen to check your work. Which words are contracted? Repeat the questions, paying attention to contractions.

6 **Pair Work** Ask each other the questions from Exercise 5a. Tell the class two things you learned about your partner.

Do you think you'll still be studying English a year from now?

I'm not sure. I think . . .

Listening

7 ▶ 1.19 Listen to two telephone conversations. What are the speakers' relationships? What plans are they trying to make?

8 We use vague or imprecise expressions when we don't want to (or can't) give details. Listen to the conversations again and listen for the expressions in the How To box.

How To:

Generalize

Give imprecise information about how often something happens	• *once in a while* • *every so often*
Give imprecise information about quantity, time, and/or numbers	• *pretty much (all day)* • *tons of mistakes* • *about eight-ish* • *in an hour or so*
Give imprecise information about things you do/have been doing	• *that kind of thing* • *the usual*
Give imprecise answers to direct questions	• *sort of* or *kind of*

9 Put the words in the correct order to make sentences. Start with the underlined word.

1. <u>We</u> go so every to that still often café.
2. <u>I'm</u> busy weekend sort this of.
3. <u>Her</u> job solving thing that kind and involves problems of.
4. <u>I'll</u> working much be pretty evening all.
5. <u>Because</u> I'm a in busy, I while so see my sister once only.
6. <u>By</u> time tons next new I'll have this of met year, people.
7. <u>We're</u> at about hoping meet four-ish to.
8. <u>I'll</u> at or arriving so ten be.

10 **Pair Work** Ask and answer the questions. Try to include generalizations in your answers.

1. How many phone calls do you make each day?
2. How many times do you check email each week?
3. How many close friends do you have?
4. How often do you write letters?
5. What do you do in the evening?
6. How many hours do you study English each day?

Speaking

11 **Pair Work** Play *Twenty Questions*. Follow the instructions in the box.

Does your person appear on TV?

Yes, every so often.

Twenty Questions

- Think of a famous person. Don't tell your partner who it is.
- Try to find out who your partner is thinking of. Ask only *yes/no* questions.
- You can ask up to 20 questions. You can generalize in your answers if you like.

LESSON 3

Follow an extended piece of discourse

CAN DO

GRAMMAR subject/verb inversion

Vocabulary | special abilities

1 **Pair Work** What are some things that most children can do by the time they are two years old? Five years old? Ten years old? Do you know of any children who developed special talents at an early age?

2 Match the words or phrases on the left to those with a similar meaning on the right.

____ 1. gifted	a. for the future
____ 2. in the making	b. difficult
____ 3. a prodigy	c. someone who is abnormal
____ 4. adulation	d. extremely talented
____ 5. peers	e. admiration
____ 6. demanding	f. a young genius
____ 7. a freak	g. contemporaries

3 Read the article and answer the questions that follow.

HOW TO MAKE YOUR CHILD A GENIUS

1 Nguyen Ngoc Truong Son grew up watching his mother and father playing chess in their home in Kien Giang Province in Vietnam. When he was three years old, he asked them to let him play, too. Expecting him to strew the pieces around the room, they gave in. Not for one minute had they imagined that their son would be able to play. Not only did Son know how to set up the chessboard, but he had also learned many rules of the game by watching them. It took Son about a month to surpass his parents. By the time he was four, Son was competing in national tournaments against children who were much older. By the age of seven, he was winning tournaments. In 2004, Son became Vietnam's youngest grandmaster ever, and one of the youngest grandmasters in the history of chess.

2 Son's parents, who are teachers, are at a loss to explain their son's talents. "It's an inborn gift," says his father. "You couldn't train an ordinary three-year-old to play like that." For Son, there is nothing unusual about his skill. The strategies and logic of chess come naturally to him. "I just see things on the board and know what to do," he says. "It's just always made sense to me."

3 Scientists have never been able to understand how child prodigies like Son acquire their talents. Prodigies have been celebrated throughout history. Rarely, however, have they been understood. As often is the case with something not easily understood, they have also been objects of suspicion and superstition. They often must deal with teasing by other children, attention from the press, and pressure and high expectations from their parents.

4 The eternal question regarding prodigies is that of nature vs. nurture. In other words, are prodigies born with their special talents, or are their environment and upbringing responsible? Only recently has science begun to investigate the cultural and biological factors that contribute to the making of child prodigies. Unfortunately, there are still no easy answers. Studies have shown that raw intelligence, as measured through IQ tests, is very heritable, that is, tends to be inherited from one's parents and grandparents. But there is not always a connection between high intelligence and the skills of prodigies. Prodigies master very specific skills. Nowhere is this illustrated more clearly than in the case of Indian prodigy Tathagat Avatar Tulsi. At the age of six, when given any date in history, he was able to immediately calculate which day of the week it was. The press nicknamed him "Computer Brain." Tulsi's talent is a type of intelligence that cannot be inherited.

5 However, there is one point on which the experts can agree: a child's upbringing has an enormous impact on whether a gift is developed or not. As Wu Wu-tien, a Taiwanese education specialist puts it, "Prodigies are half born, half made." Parents provide environments conducive to learning. They read to their children from an early age. They stimulate their brains, engage them in discussion, and foster their talents.

1. Why were Son's parents surprised?
2. What does Son think of his gift?
3. According to the article, what problems do child prodigies face?
4. What is "the big question" about child prodigies?
5. What answer does the article suggest?

4 **Pair Work** Discuss.

1. Think about other child geniuses. How do you think society treats them?
2. What might be some benefits and drawbacks of having a child prodigy in the family?
3. Do you know any children who have a special gift for something?
4. Do you think child prodigies are "born" or "made"?

Grammar | subject/verb inversion

5 Complete the tasks in the Active Grammar box.

Active Grammar

1. Inversion is used to emphasize the adverbial phrase in a sentence and to add variety to a text. Inversion is usually used in more formal writing.

   Place a negative or adverbial expression at the start of a sentence (*never*, *nowhere*, *not only*, etc.) followed by auxiliary verb + subject + verb.

   He plays *football and tennis.* → ***Not only does he play*** *football, but he also plays tennis.*

   He arrived *and we left immediately.* → ***No sooner did he arrive*** *than we left.*

2. The article on page 50 contains the following examples of inversion. Find two other examples.

   Not for one minute ***had they imagined*** *that their son would be able to play.*

   Not only ***did Son know*** *how to set up the chessboard, but he had also learned many rules of the game.*

   Rarely, however, ***have they been*** *understood.*

3. Do not use auxiliary verbs when the main verb is the verb *be* or a modal verb.

   He is a great singer and can also dance. ***Not only is he*** *a great singer,* ***but*** *he can also dance.*

Match the rules with the sentences a–d below:

____ 1. We use inversion after phrases that use *not*.

____ 2. We use inversion after negative adverbs that emphasize a time relationship.

____ 3. We use inversion for general emphasis with phrases that use *only*.

____ 4. We use inversion with *no way* in informal speech.

a. ***No way*** *am I going to sing in public!*

b. ***Only if*** *we start to play more intelligently will we win this game.*

c. ***Not since*** *I was a child have I enjoyed myself so much.*

d. ***No sooner*** *had I arrived than I had to go out again.*

See Reference page 70

6 Circle the letter of the correct sentence in each pair.

1. a. Not since Mozart there has been a greater genius.
   b. Not since Mozart has there been a greater genius.
2. a. Only after the age of three did she begin to show her gift.
   b. Only after the age of three she did begin to show her gift.
3. a. Nowhere do the rules say you can't teach advanced subjects to children.
   b. Nowhere the rules say you can't teach advanced subjects to children.
4. a. Only later did we understand the truth about our gifted child.
   b. Only later we understood the truth about our gifted child.
5. a. Not only he was able to write poetry when he was five years old; he also played the violin well.
   b. Not only was he able to write poetry when he was five years old; he also played the violin well.
6. a. No sooner had we given her a paintbrush than she produced a masterpiece.
   b. No sooner had we given her a paintbrush, she produced a masterpiece.

Speaking

7a **SPEAKING EXCHANGE** Student A: read the paragraph on page 73. Student B: read the paragraph on page 74. Complete the paragraphs, and then make notes on the following:

- name
- special talent
- what others think of him or her

b Tell your partner about the person.

Listening

8a You are going to listen to a description of two very gifted children. Before listening, read the notes below.

<u>People</u>

1. The case involved twins named ________________.
2. They were ____________ and wore thick glasses.
3. At school, people ____________ at them.

<u>Their gifts</u>

4. They could tell you ____________ in the past and future 40,000 years.
5. They could remember long sequences of ____________.
6. If you asked them about a day in their lives, they could remember ________________.

<u>Conclusions</u>

7. Their ability is mathematical and ____________.
8. When asked how they do it, they reply, "________________________."

b ▶1.20 Listen and complete the sentences.

9 **Group Work** Discuss.

1. In which jobs would the twins' abilities be useful?
2. How else could they use their abilities?
3. If you could have one special mental ability (memorizing numbers or words, having a photographic memory, being able to read extremely quickly, being able to learn many foreign languages quickly, etc.), what would it be? Why?

If I could have one special mental ability, I would like to be able to read extremely quickly. That way I could . . .

Writing

10 Write a summary of John and Michael's story.

Extra Vocabulary Study and Extra Listening Activity in ACTIVEBOOK

Review

1 Rewrite the sentences in three different ways, using the words in parentheses.

1. We expect the weather to improve in the coming months. (chance/distinct/well)
2. I doubt if they will contact us. (remote/probably/slim)
3. We will almost certainly move in the spring. (likelihood/chance/bound)
4. I don't believe they will offer him the job. (doubt/chance/distinct)
5. The organizers are confident that attendance will be high this year. (presumably/bound/strong)

2 Circle the correct words.

1. Max *will retire/is retired/will retiring* soon, so we *'ll be looking/look/will be look* for a new manager.
2. Wait a minute. I'm *coming/will come/will be coming*.
3. By this time next year, he *'s going to be/'ll be/is* in college.
4. Will you *going to see/have seen/be seeing* Jade this week?
5. Don't worry if you haven't finished. I *'m working/'m going to work/work* on it later.
6. I'm sure he *'ll be getting/will have gotten/is getting* a job by the end of the year.

3 Circle the correct choice.

1. No sooner ____ left the airport than I realized I had picked up the wrong suitcase.
   a. did I b. had I c. would I
2. No ____ should you be made to pay the difference.
   a. means b. cases c. way
3. Not ____ did they think it would be possible.
   a. for once b. for one minute c. for ever
4. Only if you practice ____.
   a. you will get better b. would you get better c. will you get better
5. It is not often ____ such a difficult question.
   a. that am I asked b. that I am asked c. do I ask

4 Use the cues in parentheses and the phrases in the box to complete the sentences.

pretty much	in a while	every so often	came up
fell through	up to	swamped	free

1. I see her once ____________________. (very occasionally)
2. I'm ____________________. (have nothing to do)
3. What are you ____________________ tomorrow? (doing)
4. I'm ____________________ finished. (nearly)
5. A few problems ____________________ yesterday. (appeared)
6. I still go to that restaurant ____________________. (not regularly)
7. I am totally ____________________ right now. (very busy)
8. The dinner ____________________. (was cancelled)

Communication | make an argument for research funding

5 1.21 Listen to four speakers talking about important discoveries and inventions. Answer the questions.

1. What technologies do they mention, and what do they say about them?
2. What other important discoveries or inventions can you think of?
3. How have they changed our lives or made the world a better place?

6 **Pair Work** Read the paragraphs and answer the following questions.

1. Is each area of research likely to affect your life?
2. Would you contribute money to research in this area?

Space travel/exploration

NASA has spent billions of dollars every year to send astronauts into space. Now Virgin Galactic is offering to take private citizens into space. They have already collected $6 million in deposits. For $200,000, the paying public will fly 70 miles above the Earth, see the planet's curvature, and experience weightlessness for at least six minutes.

Robots

Various domestic robots are available to do your ironing, mow the lawn, vacuum, etc. Now, some hospitals are experimenting with robo-docs so that doctors can "visit" patients from a distance (another ward, or even specialists from another country). Also, scientists are improving robots for space exploration.

Genetic engineering

Using DNA, scientists can now manipulate the development of life. In 2001 a cloned cat named "Little Nicky" was sold to a Texan woman for $50,000. Now scientists are researching the use of DNA to predict hereditary illnesses in unborn babies. The scientists could then potentially alter the babies' genes to prevent the illnesses. Many people worry that the techniques will be used commercially, for example, to manufacture "superchildren" with unnatural physical advantages.

7a **Group Work** Prepare a case for research funding. Group A: prepare a case for research into space travel; Group B: prepare a case for research into how robots can help mankind; Group C: prepare a case for research into genetic engineering. First, discuss the questions below:

1. What important discoveries do you think might be made in this area in the future?
2. What do you think is needed to make this research possible?
3. How do you think the research should be funded?
4. How will the research affect people's lives?

b Present your ideas to the rest of the class. Discuss which arguments you found persuasive.

UNIT 5
Making money

A

B

C

D

Warm Up

1 **Pair Work** Discuss the meaning of the words and phrases in bold in the sentences below. Can any of them be used to describe the photos?

1. She **came into a fortune** when she turned 18.
2. They **haggled** to get a good deal.
3. The **stock market** is often unpredictable.
4. The employees have asked for a **raise**.
5. The taxes will affect **high-income** families.
6. John Singer Sargent's paintings are **priceless**.
7. The sales force is **paid on commission**.
8. Unfortunately, his business **went bankrupt** last year.

2 **Pair Work** Do you agree with the statements below? Give reasons for your answers.

1. Art belongs to everyone. Priceless paintings should be available for all to see.
2. It's rude to haggle when you buy something. You should pay the asking price.
3. Paying people on a commission basis makes them work hard.
4. High-income families should pay higher taxes.
5. Gambling on the stock market is a sure way to go bankrupt.
6. The best way to get a raise is to be nice to your boss.

Talk about professional relationships

GRAMMAR emphasis

Reading

1 **Pair Work** Discuss.

1. How important do you think it is for an employer to make sure that his or her employees are happy? Why?
2. What kinds of things do you think employers can reasonably do to increase employee satisfaction?

2 Read the article and answer the questions that follow.

Zingerman's Community of Businesses

1 Sink your teeth into a Zingerman's Reuben Sandwich—corned beef, Swiss cheese, sauerkraut, and Russian dressing on grilled rye bread—and you will get a new appreciation for the word *sandwich*. Zingerman's Deli in Ann Arbor, Michigan, has over 100 varieties of delicious sandwiches, all made on homemade breads and packed with the freshest local ingredients. It's no wonder it's been called the best deli in the world! But it's not only the menu at Zingerman's that is exceptional. The Zingerman's business model is also something to learn from.

2 Founded in 1982 by Paul Saginaw and Ari Weinzweig, Zingerman's began as a unique little delicatessen serving a modest number of traditional deli dishes and sandwiches. It rapidly grew in popularity, with customers often waiting in long lines to sample one of the infamous sandwiches. The potential for bigger success was clear. It was Saginaw who suggested franchising nationwide. But Weinzweig was not the least bit interested in expanding geographically and compromising the uniqueness and purpose of the original deli. He also preferred that they stay in their own neighborhood. So they chose a different, more unusual route. They started building other businesses around Zingerman's Deli, all located in the Ann Arbor area: a bake house, a creamery, a mail order, a coffee company, among others. Each business is run by one or more managing partners who share ownership and oversee the daily operations. All the businesses fall under the umbrella of Zingerman's Community of Businesses (ZCoB).

3 What is unique about ZCoB is that anyone can pitch an idea for a business and potentially become a member of the Zingerman's community. Several of the businesses were founded by Zingerman's employees. In general, at Zingerman's input from employees is highly encouraged and valued. And they are generously rewarded for their efforts. It's a work environment where people truly thrive. Zingerman's employees really do love coming to work. "It actually doesn't feel like work at all," shares one employee. ZCoB also provides excellent compensation and benefits, including generous vacation time, health and dental benefits, food discounts, and various incentive plans for full-time employees. But everyone agrees that it's the Zingerman's environment that is priceless. Many talented employees have left much higher paying jobs to be part of the unique Zingerman's experience.

4 So what's the secret? Zingerman's business model measures success based on great food, great service, and financial results. But this is by no means a secret. Quite on the contrary, ZingTrain, the training branch of the company, offers business training and consulting to share Zingerman's philosophies and their people-friendly management approach. So managers from grocery chains, banks, hospitals, and garden shops from across the country gather regularly in Ann Arbor for seminars on how to improve their businesses. Those who can't travel to Michigan can read about the Zingerman's culture and structure in Ari Weinzweig's book *A Lapsed Anarchist's Approach to Building a Great Business*. He readily shares the ingredients for making a unique, successful, and lasting business.

5 That in itself is perhaps what makes Zingerman's such a success—the readiness to share their wealth. And just as they don't keep their business model a secret, they don't keep the recipe for their Reuben Sandwich under lock and key. You can go to the Zingerman's mail order at zingerman's.com and find detailed step-by-step instructions for making the sandwich. And if you want to splurge, you can actually order a Reuben Sandwich Kit. It includes every single ingredient for the sandwich, from the thick slices of homemade bread to the Russian dressing—just like you would get at Zingerman's deli. Now that's great food and great service!

1. What kind of business is Zingerman's?
2. How has the company changed since 1982?
3. What are some of the things that make Zingerman's different from more traditional businesses?
4. How does Zingerman's measure success?
5. Why do managers from other companies come to Zingerman's for training?

3 **Pair Work** Discuss the meaning of the words and phrases from the reading in bold.

1. The **potential** for bigger success was clear. (paragraph 2)
2. Weinzweig was not interested in **compromising** the uniqueness of the original deli. (paragraph 2)
3. Anyone can **pitch an idea** for a business. (paragraph 3)
4. It's a work environment where people truly **thrive**. (paragraph 3)
5. ZCoB provides excellent **compensation and benefits**, including generous vacation time, health and dental benefits, food discounts, and various **incentive plans**. (paragraph 3)
6. ZingTrain offers business training and consulting to share Zingerman's **philosophies**. (paragraph 4)

Grammar | emphasis

4 Complete the task after each rule in the Active Grammar box.

Active Grammar

We can add emphasis by including certain words, for example:

1. *own*—to intensify possessive adjectives
   Find an example in paragraph 2.
2. emphasizing negatives: *the least bit/at all*
   Find examples in paragraphs 2 and 3.
3. adjectives/adverbs to add emphasis: *actually, by no means, even*
   Find examples in paragraphs 3, 4, and 5.
4. auxiliary verbs: *do/did*
   Find an example in paragraph 3.

We can use cleft sentences for emphasis. Two important cleft constructions are:

5. *it* clauses
   It was Scott who asked . . .
   Find examples in paragraphs 2 and 3.
6. *what* clauses
   What you need is a cup of coffee . . .
   Find an example in paragraph 3.

See Reference page 71

5a Rewrite the sentences to add emphasis using the words in parentheses.

1. He can't complain. It's his fault he didn't get a raise. (own)
2. We're not certain that it is the same man committing the crimes. (by)
3. I really miss having enough time to spend with friends. (what)
4. They didn't understand what we wanted. (all)
5. The employees love coming to work. (actually)
6. Sammy always got into trouble. (it)
7. Keith wasn't annoyed when we cancelled the meeting. (least)

American English	British English
a raise	*a rise*

b ▶1.22 Listen to the answers. Mark the words that are stressed. Practice saying the sentences with the same stress and intonation.

Speaking

6 **Pair Work** Discuss. Use emphasis where possible.

1. What do you think the three most important elements of a successful business are?
2. Would you consider starting your own business? Why or why not?
3. Who would or wouldn't you choose for a business partner? Why?

Listening

7 1.23 Listen and complete the sentences.

1. The speaker warns against doing business with ______________.
2. The only way to get rid of a bad business partner legally is to ______________.
3. Successful partnerships will combine two types of people: __________ and __________.
4. It's a good idea if partners have complementary __________.
5. If your business is lacking in a particular skill area, you may need to ______________.
6. Good __________ is essential to ensure that arguments do not interfere with the success of the business.
7. Ideally, your business partner will be committed to the __________ success of the business.

8a 1.24 Listen again in sections. As you listen, notice how the speaker uses the following phrases:

Section 1	*50-50 partners, family-owned business, make someone a partner, buy someone out of the business, an expensive proposition*
Section 2	*a strategic "big picture" thinker, business model, plan, roll up their sleeves, execute the strategy, strike the right balance, strategy and tactics*
Section 3	*make the business work, product design, marketing background, crunch the numbers, contract negotiation, bookkeeping, hire a consultant*
Section 4	*communicate directly and honestly, business may suffer, hold back information, jeopardize the friendship*
Section 5	*start-up phase, an attractive job offer, a life-changing event, the going gets tough*

b **Pair Work** Check that you understand the meaning of the phrases from Exercise 8a. Then reconstruct the speaker's advice, using those phrases and the information from Exercise 7.

9 **Group Work** Discuss.

1. Do you agree with what the speaker says? Do you know people in successful or unsuccessful business partnerships? Why do you think the relationship does or doesn't work?
2. Are you a "visionary" or an "operations" person? What skills, experience and qualities would you bring to a business partnership? In which areas are you lacking? Would you work well with the other students in your group?

I guess I'm a "visionary." I'm really good at coming up with ideas, but I'm not great at organizing . . .

LESSON 2

Discuss financial decisions and regrets

CAN DO

GRAMMAR conditionals: review

Reading

1 **Pair Work** Read the quotes below. Which do you agree or disagree with?

"There are a million ways to make money and a billion ways to lose it."

"Money is only a tool. It will take you wherever you wish, but it will not replace you as the driver."

2a **SPEAKING EXCHANGE** Work in pairs. Student A: read about Leon Spinks on this page. Student B: read about William Post on page 75. Make notes about the following as you read:

1. How did he win his money? How much was it?
2. How did he lose his money?
3. What does he do now?
4. What kind of relationship does or did he have with his family?
5. What "philosophy" does each man express at the end of the article?

Reading A

RICHES TO RAGS

Leon Spinks, the former heavyweight boxing champion who famously beat Muhammad Ali in a 1978 fight, has had a hard fall from glory. Once known for his wild partying and extravagant lifestyle, Spinks now works at a McDonald's and volunteers at an after-school program for kids in the small town of Columbus, Nebraska. "I love helping the kids," he says. To many of them, he is still a hero.

Spinks was at the height of his fame in the late 1970s. In 1976, both he and his younger brother Michael won gold medals at the Olympics in Montreal. "That will always be my greatest achievement," Spinks says. But he is best known for his win over Ali in 1978.

The good times did not last long, however. In the seven months between his victory and his next match with Ali, Spinks lost the self-control that had propelled him to the championship. He partied and neglected his training. He lost his next bout with Ali, and his life spiraled downward from there. He continued to box until 1995, but never again at the same level.

Spinks made millions from boxing, but the common perception is that he partied away all of his money. Spinks says the truth is that he trusted the wrong people. He gave power of attorney to his lawyers and says that he never saw a penny of the $3.25 million that he made from Ali-Spinks 2. Eventually the money was gone, and for a brief period he was homeless. Spinks lived for a while in Chicago and from there moved to Columbus, where he works for minimum wage and lives quietly.

Spinks's brother Michael did not make the same mistakes as Leon. When Michael beat Larry Holmes in 1985, the Spinks boys became the first brothers to become world heavyweight champions. But unlike his brother, Michael held on to his money. "My brother and I are close," Leon says. But he will not ask for financial help. "I can make it myself."

Spinks still carries himself with dignity, though he does worry about the future and whether he will have enough money to live comfortably. "You do the best you can," he says. "I'm still trying. I'm not giving up on life."

b Tell your partner about the person in your reading.

3a Find words and phrases in the readings from Exercise 2 that mean the following:

1. ______________________: offer to work (usually for no money) (Reading A)
2. ______________________: the power to make legal decisions regarding finances (Reading A)
3. ______________________: didn't receive any of the money (Reading A)
4. ______________________: got worse and worse (Reading A)
5. ______________________: take someone to court to get money from them (Reading B)
6. ______________________: new business activities (Reading B)
7. ______________________: declare that you are unable to pay your debts (Reading B)

b Complete the sentences with a phrase from Exercise 3a.

1. He's made a lot of money with his new __________ __________.
2. She said she would send a check, but I still haven't __________ __________ __________ of the money she owes us.
3. Steve has __________ to help me sort out the office.
4. The business had been failing for years before he __________ __________.

Grammar | conditionals: review

4 Complete the sentences with the correct form of the verb in parentheses.

Ex: If you go into business with relatives, it *tends to* (tend to) put a strain on your relationship.

1. If you happen to ____________ (see) Tom, could you tell him I need some money?
2. I wish I ____________ (not gamble) with the money.
3. She wouldn't have been able to pay her debts if she ____________ (not come into) a lot of money.
4. They wouldn't have ____________ (be able) to buy the house if it hadn't been for her father.
5. He shouldn't have to declare bankruptcy, provided the business ventures ____________ (be) successful.
6. If you ____________ (like) to follow me, I'll show you to your rooms.
7. We'd be rich now if we ____________ (not lost) the ticket.
8. ____________ (shall) you have any questions, please do not hesitate to contact me.
9. If only he ____________ (stop) pestering me, I'd try to help.

5 Complete the sentences in the Active Grammar box with the correct phrase.

Active Grammar

a. if it hadn't been for . . .	1. ____ can be used with real conditional sentences to emphasize that something is unlikely to occur.
b. should you . . .	2. ____ can be used instead of *if* to show that specific conditions should be met for something to happen.
c. provided (that) . . ./as long as . . .	3. ____ is often used to show that a negative result would have occurred without a certain person or event.
d. if only . . .	4. ____ can be used to express a wish or regret.
e. happen to/should happen to . . .	5. ____ is often used in formal business communication.
f. if you will/would . . .	6. ____ can be used as a polite form.

See Reference page 71

6 Use the prompts in parentheses to rewrite the sentences so the meaning stays the same.

Ex: I'll renew the contract if the conditions stay the same. (provided)

I'll renew the contract provided the conditions stay the same.

1. I failed the exam because the last question was so difficult. (if it . . . passed the exam)
2. I didn't have my credit card with me so I didn't buy any presents. (I would . . .)
3. The business isn't doing well because there is so much competition. (if only . . . better)
4. Thanks to Dr. Crane, I recovered quickly. (if it . . . might not)
5. They argued about money, and their partnership broke up. (if they . . . business partners now.)

Speaking

7 **Group Work** Discuss, using conditionals.

1. What would you do if only you had more time?
2. If you happened to win $1,000, what would you do with it?
3. Is there anything that you wish you had done when you were younger?

Reading

8 Read the article and circle the correct choices.

GREAT PHILANTHROPISTS

Andrew Carnegie

Can you imagine becoming the richest person in the world, and then giving all your money away? That's exactly what Andrew Carnegie did. Carnegie made millions of dollars during his highly successful business career. As a result, when he retired in 1901, at the age of 66, he was the world's richest man. But Carnegie outlined his beliefs about wealth in an essay, "The Gospel of Wealth." In the essay, he describes how wealthy men ought to live without (**1.** _greedy / charity / money / extravagance_), provide moderately (**2.** _of / for / on / to_) their families, and consider the rest of their wealth as extra money that should be distributed to promote the (**3.** _welfare / farewell / sickness / richness_) and happiness of other people. "The Gospel of Wealth" was read all over the world, and Carnegie's worthy intentions were praised. Very wealthy people of that period lived (**4.** _greatly / lavishly / hugely / cheaply_) and spent huge amounts of money on their own personal needs and wishes, but Andrew Carnegie was not one of them. In his lifetime, he gave away more than $350 million or almost 90 percent of his (**5.** _treasure / fortune / collection / account_) for what he considered to be the improvement of all mankind.

But he wasn't the only generous American of his time. John D. Rockefeller once said, "Giving away money intelligently is more difficult than making it." Having given away $530 million to (**6.** _care / help / charity / cause_), he should know.

Rockefeller's entrepreneurial skills started when he was young. When he was just 12 years old, he lent $50 to a farmer. The following year, he got the money back and (**7.** _charged / asked / insisted / paid_) interest! But his philanthropic journey was inspired by the tragic death of his three-year-old grandson. When the boy died of scarlet fever, Rockefeller began putting his money (**8.** _onto / in / into / to_) medical research. He (**9.** _foundation / founded / found / foundered_) the Rockefeller Institute in 1901, and later his doctors became famous for flying around the world providing vaccines for children.

Helping children is a (**10.** _mission / missive / work / problem_) close to the heart of another pair of famous philanthropists, Bill and Melinda Gates. Gates not only earns but also gives away more money than anyone else in the world. The Bill and Melinda Gates Foundation has saved 700,000 children's lives through its health programs. Gates (**11.** _puts / spends / dedicates / creates_) billions to fighting diseases like malaria, which are still killers in the developing world. Closer to home, he has set up education programs and scholarship funds designed to have a major (**12.** _change / affect / result / impact_) on children growing up in the US.

While we can (**13.** _inspire / admire / cope / afford_) the generosity and (**14.** _idea / visual / ambitious / vision_) of all these people, perhaps we should leave the last word to Rockefeller's colleague, Raymond Fosdick. He wrote that it's a mistake to think "that money can create ideas, and that a great (**15.** _amounts / sum / deal / lot_) of money can create better ideas. You cannot buy scientists or poets."

Bill and Melinda Gates

9 **Pair Work** Discuss the questions.

1. Which charities do you/would you support, and why?
2. "Tragedy often inspires generosity." Would you agree?
3. "You cannot buy scientists or poets." Do you agree? Why or why not?

I volunteer for a local charity that delivers food to the homeless. It . . .

Express priorities

GRAMMAR sentence adverbials

How To:

Express priorities

Saying it's very important	• *My first priority is . . .* • *The essential thing for me is . . .* • *____ is vital.* • *I couldn't do without . . .*
Saying it's not important	• *I'm not really concerned about . . .* • *It isn't a major priority.* • *I could do without . . .*

Speaking

1 **Pair Work** Think about what is important in a job. Then discuss which items in the box are priorities for you. Try to use some of the expressions from the How To box.

opportunity for promotion	401K
flexible working hours	benefits
convenient location	good salary
professional development	job satisfaction
working environment	freedom/autonomy
supportive colleagues/manager	challenging work

American English	British English
flexible working hours	*flexitime*

Reading

2 Read the article and answer the questions that follow.

TOP COMPANIES

Every year since 1998, *Fortune* Magazine has published a list of the "100 Best Companies to Work For." How does the magazine choose the companies? First, it uses a survey: 350 employees answer 57 questions about their company. Second, it looks at important features of companies; for example, pay, benefits, and communication between workers and management.

To a certain extent, the results are guesswork, but the companies on the list, by and large, have many things in common: they pay their employees well, they allow workers to make decisions, and they offer a comfortable workplace. Broadly speaking, however, the winners tend to offer something above and beyond the norm. J. M. Smucker, a jam and jelly company, gives its workers free muffins and bagels for breakfast; at Griffin Hospital, employees get free massages; a bank called First Horizon National gives its employees time off to visit their children's classrooms. Wegmans Food Markets sent one worker on a ten-day trip to London, Paris, and Italy to learn about cheese. This is not unusual for the New York-based company, which is well-known for the scholarships it gives its employees to further their education. At W. L. Gore, workers decide on their colleagues' salaries. Surprisingly enough, the most important thing for the majority of employees is not money. It is the freedom to develop ideas. Timberland offers a six-month paid sabbatical for employees who have "a personal dream that benefits the community."

Let's not forget that all these companies are businesses whose priority is making money. They have to make a profit. And do they? Seemingly, the answer is a big "yes." The number three company on *Fortune's* 2011 list, Wegmans, makes a fortune. The company, which has a motto, "Employees first, customers second," is one of the 50 largest private companies in the US, with annual sales of $3.6 billion, according to *Forbes* magazine. Apparently, being good to your employees is no obstacle to making money.

How much of Wegmans' success is due to the company's policies? "Up to a point, the success is because of the freedom they give us," says one employee. "On the other hand, no company gets rich just by being nice. Wegmans has great marketing strategies, and it's well-positioned within the community. I've been here for 15 years. Looking back, I'd say that the company's innovations for customers, such as the Shoppers' Club electronic discount program in the '90s, have been just as important as the benefits to staff."

But the employee benefits are striking. Fundamentally, Wegmans believes in professional development. In addition to scholarships, the company gives its employees business opportunities. For years, one employee made delicious cookies for her colleagues. Eventually, she started selling the cookies in Wegmans. "I just asked the manager," she says. "In hindsight, I should have asked earlier. I could have made more money!"

The staff's freedom to make decisions is another thing you won't find everywhere. Essentially, Wegmans wants its workers to do almost anything to keep its customers happy. Believe it or not, an employee once cooked a Thanksgiving turkey in the store for a customer because the woman's turkey, bought at Wegmans, was too big for her oven. One manager says, "We're a $3 billion company run by 16-year-old cashiers."

1. How does *Fortune* Magazine get the results for its annual list?
2. What makes the winners special?
3. What is Wegmans' philosophy?
4. Why does a manager say that the company is run by 16-year-old cashiers?

Grammar | sentence adverbials

3 Read the article on page 62 again. What purpose do the underlined words and phrases serve? Complete the tasks in the Active Grammar box.

Active Grammar

Circle the correct choice to complete the rules below.

1. Sentence adverbials show how the sentence fits in with the rest of the text, and frequently go at the beginning / middle / end of a sentence.
2. Sentence adverbials show the speaker's attitude and feelings, and are usually separated from the rest of the sentence by a period / comma.

Complete the chart using the underlined examples in the article on page 62.

Adverbial Functions	Examples
Basic ideas	*fundamentally, essentially*
Generalizations	
How something appears	
Contrast	
Reflection on the past	
Partial agreement	

Add any other adverbial phrases that you can think of to the chart.

See Reference page 71

4 Circle the two sentence adverbials that fit the context of each sentence.

Ex: *We want our workers to be happy. ____, this means helping them foster a sense of pride in their work.*

(a. Fundamentally) (b. Essentially) c. With hindsight

1. We believe in giving our employees as much autonomy as possible. ____, we try not to interfere unless really necessary.
   a. Broadly speaking b. Apparently c. By and large
2. Our employees don't complain if they have to work on weekends. ____, they do expect to be paid overtime for it.
   a. On the other hand b. Seemingly c. However
3. We believe in second chances, because employees learn from their mistakes. ____, our company has never fired an employee.
   a. Believe it or not b. Surprisingly enough c. Broadly speaking
4. Employees help set salaries ____, but they are not allowed to pay themselves unreasonable amounts.
   a. up to a point b. apparently c. to a certain extent
5. Some employees' salaries were getting too high. ____, we should have introduced a pay cap earlier.
   a. Believe it or not b. Looking back c. In hindsight

Speaking

5 **Group Work** Discuss whether you agree or disagree with the statements.

1. It's a good idea for employees to set their own salaries.
2. Employees shouldn't have to wear uniforms.
3. Employees should be allowed to evaluate their managers.
4. In the future, everyone will have flexible work schedules.

I don't think it's a good idea for employees to set their own salaries, unless there's some way to control how high they get . . .

I'm not so sure. I think employees might be more invested in the success of the company if they're part of the decision-making process.

Listing

6a **Pair Work** Discuss. Do you know of any companies with particularly good or bad working conditions? What effect do the conditions have on the employees and on the company's success?

b ▶1.25 Listen to an interview. Then discuss the questions.

1. What do you think of the ideas introduced at Blue Skies Recruitment? Would you like to work for the company? Why or why not?
2. If you were the director of a new company, what ideas would you introduce to help retain your staff?

Vocabulary | expressing quantity

handful	plenty	most	few	bit
majority	many	much	deal	

7a Complete the phrases from the listening, using the words in the box.

1. as ____________ as (a surprisingly large number)
2. a little ____________ more (a little more)
3. a great ____________ of energy (a lot of energy)
4. ____________ of benefits (a lot of benefits)
5. not ____________ of an expert (not really an expert)
6. for the ____________ part (generally)
7. the vast ____________ (most of)
8. quite a ____________ employees (a large number)
9. only a ____________ of people (very few people)

b ▶1.26 Listen to check your answers.

8 Rewrite the sentences using the words in parentheses.

1. The government spends a lot of money on defense.
   The government . . . (great)
2. The customers generally appreciate our top-quality service.
   For . . . (most)
3. There's more than enough room.
   There . . . (plenty)
4. It isn't a huge fee if you consider the amount of work involved.
   It . . . (much)
5. Three or four people asked questions.
   Only . . . (handful)
6. Most of the workers joined the strike.
   The . . . (vast)

9a Complete the sentences using phrases from Exercise 7.

Ex: I think the government wastes . . . on . . . *I think the government wastes a great deal of money on inefficient projects.*

1. There are . . . women in top management positions because . . .
2. . . . of people in this country . . .
3. I spend . . . my time . . .
4. . . . of road accidents could be avoided if . . .
5. There are not . . . as there used to be.

b **Pair Work** Discuss your sentences with a partner. Do you agree with your partner's opinions?

Writing

10 Choose one of the sentences in Exercise 9a and write a paragraph on the topic.

Extra Vocabulary Study and Extra Listening Activity in ACTIVEBOOK

Review

1 Rewrite the sentences using the correct option in parentheses. There may be more than one possibility.

1. He was offered the job, but he didn't accept it. (surprisingly enough/broadly speaking)
2. They explained how the project would be too difficult to manage, and I agree. (on the other hand/ to a certain extent)
3. They didn't know who I was talking about. Georgia left the company years ago. (Principally/Apparently)
4. I decided to change careers. I'm not sure that I made the right decision. (Essentially/In hindsight)
5. The new arrangements have worked out well. (By and large/Primarily)
6. The new president was faced with an impossible task. (however/seemingly)

2 Cross out the clause that cannot be used to complete each sentence.

1. If he'd planned to give the money back, why ____
   a. didn't he contact the police?
   b. hadn't he contact the police?
   c. would he contact the police?
2. If you lost your job tomorrow, ____
   a. what are you going to do?
   b. what would you do?
   c. you could call me.
3. He can come with us provided that ____
   a. he pays for his own meals.
   b. he would pay for his room.
   c. he doesn't drive the car.
4. If you happen to find my bag, ____
   a. could you call this number?
   b. just give it to Sue.
   c. I'd be really surprised.
5. If it hadn't been for Mary, ____
   a. you will still be waiting.
   b. we would never have found you.
   c. everything would have been fine.

3 Rewrite the sentences using the words in parentheses for emphasis.

1. We weren't at all surprised to hear that she got the part. (bit)
2. I think it is surprisingly warm here. (actually)
3. She makes a lot of her clothes. (own)
4. It is not certain that the game will take place. (means)
5. Rachel had the courage to complain about the service. (it)
6. They have done nothing to fix the problem. (all)

4 Complete the paragraph using the words in the box.

founded	lavishly	wealthy	vision	mind
volunteer	venture	fortune	impact	charity

Anita Cuello, who __________ (**1.**) a highly successful chain of eco-conscious clothing stores, says she plans to give away her entire __________ (**2.**) to __________ (**3.**). Ms. Cuello started her business __________ (**4.**) in 1999 with her husband. Their __________ (**5.**) was to create a line of clothing that was beautiful and stylish and that could be produced with minimal __________ (**6.**) on the environment. They succeeded beyond their wildest dreams. Now Cuello says that she has had enough of business life and hopes to achieve peace of __________ (**7.**) by sharing her good fortune with those who have not been so lucky. "I don't understand greed," she says. "I do not know why extremely __________ (**8.**) people choose to live so __________ (**9.**)." Cuello and her family live modestly and __________ (**10.**) at local charities. "Money is best when you use it to help others," she says.

Communication | negotiate

5 ▶1.27 Listen to two people discussing what they would do if their company suddenly had $1 million to spend. What ideas do they have? How are the speakers different?

6 **Group Work** What would you suggest if your company or school suddenly had $1 million to spend? Compare your ideas with other groups.

7 Read the profile of Fortune Foods and answer the questions.

1. What are the company's main strengths?
2. What are the main problems for employees?

Company Profile

Company: Fortune Foods

Product: Quality food for parties

Strengths:

- Company has an excellent reputation and is growing.
- Clients are high-end businesses.

Problems:

- Employees often stay late at night to finish preparing food.
- Employees have a high level of stress.
- Factory is in a part of the city with bad roads and heavy traffic. It is difficult to drive there.

Financial Situation: Fortune Foods made a profit last year.

8 **SPEAKING EXCHANGE** Fortune Foods has just received an investment of $2 million. Read the instructions below, and decide what the company should do with the money.

1. Work in two groups (one group represents the employees and the other represents management). Group A (employees): read page 74. Group B (management): read page 73.
2. Spend some time preparing your arguments, and then begin a negotiation with the other group.
3. Discuss. How did the negotiations go? What did you decide? Was everyone happy with the decision?

Unit 1 Reference

Verbs and adjectives with prepositions

There are many phrases that use fixed prepositions.

Verb + preposition: *opt for, distinguish from, succeed in, stem from, appeal to, bother about, rely on, benefit from*

Adjective + preposition: *short of, riddled with, lacking in, nervous about*

See page 10 for a full description of preposition use.

Passives

Passives can be used for "distancing." This means that the speaker or writer doesn't want complete responsibility for the ideas he or she expresses. The passive is often used:

- to make a statement less personal and slightly more polite.
  We don't allow that. → *That* ***isn't allowed.*** (It isn't the speaker's decision; it is an impersonal rule.)
  You must hand in the essay by Friday. → *The essay* ***must be handed*** *in by Friday.*
- in formal writing when the focus is on achievements and events rather than the people who were responsible.
  The vaccine ***was discovered*** *by chance.*

There are some common passive expressions to show that we are not certain of a statement.

It is believed that *the thief was an ex-employee.*

It is said that *he was able to speak more than 20 languages, but there is no proof.*

It was claimed that *the president hadn't seen the documents before the scandal broke out.*

She was thought *to have come from Germany originally, but there was little evidence.*

He was reported *to have been living in Brazil, but there was only one sighting of him.*

Perfect forms

Use perfect forms to refer from one point in time to another point in time before that. It shows that the speaker sees one event as 1) linked to a later event or 2) finished by a certain time.

*She****'d lost*** *her ticket, so she missed the show.*

By 6:00, I ***will have finished*** *my work.*

Use the present perfect to describe something that happened:

- during a period that includes past and present.
  *We****'ve been*** *here since 8:00 A.M.*
- in the past but when the exact time isn't relevant to this discussion or isn't known.
  *She****'s lived*** *in over 20 countries.*
- in the past but has a result or effect in the present.
  *Oh no! I****'ve lost*** *my passport.*
- in the very recent past (especially with *just*).
  I've just heard *the news.*

Use the past perfect to talk about completed actions that happened before another action in the past.

She wanted to go to the museum, but ***we'd already been*** *there.*

Use the future perfect with time phrases with *by*, for example—*by that time, by this time next week, by the end of February, by the end of the day.*

By June *we* ***will have finished*** *the project.*

Perfect forms are often used with *for*, *since*, and *just*.

By January, I ***will have been*** *here* ***for*** *a year.*

I've just been speaking *to Mickey.*

I thought it was time to move because ***I'd been living*** *there* ***since*** *1967.*

Unit Vocabulary

Challenges

have the right attitude, face challenges, rises to the challenge, set achievable goals, couldn't have done it without

Learning languages

fluent, master, pick up, dialect, linguistic ability, cram, mother tongue, universal language

Talking about knowledge

next to nothing, I'm pretty sure, inside out, I'm positive, I haven't a clue, by heart, I've never heard of him, I don't know offhand, I haven't the faintest idea, off the top of my head, like the back of my hand

Achievement

pursue, deal with, an ultimate ambition, paid off, believe in, have the potential, head (straight for the top), continue to push someone

REFERENCE

Unit 2 Reference

Gerund and infinitive review

When one verb follows another, the second verb is either a gerund or an infinitive.

Some of the verbs that are followed by a gerund are related in meaning. These verbs show personal tastes: *adore, like, don't mind, detest, can't stand*

*I **adore living** here.*

*I **can't stand listening** to their music all night.*

Other verbs take an object + infinitive. (*I told her to come here.*) Some of these verbs are also related in meaning. These verbs show one person (or thing) influencing the actions of another:
warn, tell, advise, urge, order, persuade, encourage, force, forbid, allow

*I **persuaded her to visit** me.*

*She **warned him not to go** there.*

Verbs that are followed by a preposition use the gerund:

*I **look forward to meeting** her.*

*He **succeeded in finding** a job.*

*We **insist on paying.***

Some verbs can only be followed by the infinitive or the gerund. See page 21.

Comparisons

There are many expressions that show if the difference between two things is big or small.

For a small difference use:
slightly, a little bit, a tiny bit, etc.

*I'm **slightly taller** than Peter.*

*The population is **slightly larger** than that of Ghana. (formal)*

For a large difference use:
much, far, considerably (formal), etc.

*They're **far better** than us at football.*

*The government was **considerably more** corrupt a hundred years ago. (formal)*

As + adjective + *as* means the two things are equal.

*I'm **as intelligent as** my sister.*

*It took me **as long** to drive to the city **as** it did to travel there by train.*

To indicate two things aren't equal, say:

*She's **not as big as** me. (= she's smaller)*

*The new menu **isn't as nice as** the one they had during the summer.*

There are many expressions with *as* + adjective + *as* that show whether the difference is big or small.

For a small difference use:
not quite as

*This bed is**n't quite as comfortable as** the other one. (= It's nearly as comfortable)*

For a big difference use:
nowhere near, not nearly

*He's **not nearly as good as** me at tennis.*

We can use double comparatives with *the* to say that one thing causes another.

***The longer** you take, **the less** chance we have of catching the plane.*

***The more** you write down, **the more** you'll remember.*

Unit Vocabulary

Qualities of communities

cost of living	mild climate
healthcare system	freedom
standard of living	crime rate
unemployment	pollution
cultural life	nightlife

Recommending places

a must — a must-see — Don't miss . . .
overrated — overpriced — You should try . . .
If I were you, I'd go to . . . — watch out for
Make sure you go to . . .
good value for the money
not all it's cracked up to be

Adjectives to describe places

unspoiled	diverse	off the beaten track
tranquil	vast	run-down
stunning	packed	magnificent
bustling		

Unit 3 Reference

Review of past forms

Past forms are often used together in order to make clear the order of events in a story.

Use the **simple past** to talk about completed actions in the past.

*We **went** to Paraguay last year.*

The simple past can be used for short actions, long actions, or repeated actions.

Use the **past continuous** to talk about actions in progress at a particular time in the past.

*We **were talking** about her when she walked in.*

The past continuous is often used to set the scene in a narrative.

*The sun **was shining** and the children **were playing** in the park. Suddenly . . .*

Use the **past perfect** to talk about completed actions that happened before another action in the past. The past perfect is used only to refer to two actions or moments in the past.

*She took out a DVD, but I**'d already seen** it.*

The past perfect is <u>not</u> needed to describe past events in chronological order.

*We **ordered** the food, **ate** and **paid**.*

Use the **past perfect continuous** to talk about actions or situations that continued up to the moment in the past that is being talked about.

*Before he gave up, he**'d been smoking** for years.*

The past perfect continuous is often used to show the reasons for a situation.

*He was angry because he**'d been waiting** for hours.*

Compound adjectives

Compounds frequently use a hyphen (-) between the words, but there are no definite rules about this.

Often the second word is a present or past participle.

When the first word of the compound is an adjective, the stress is often on the second word.

*far-**seeing**, strong-**willed**, slow-**moving***

When the first word of the compound is a noun, the stress is often on the first word.

***man**eating shark, **sun**tanned, **attention**-craving*

Phrases with participles and gerunds

Instead of a complete adjective clause, we can use a participial phrase:

*I recognize the man **who is sitting** over there. →*
*I recognize the man **sitting** over there.*

A full adverbial clause can be reduced to a participial phrase to express cause, result, conditions, etc. They sound formal and are more common in writing than speech.

***Because he was feeling hungry**, he bought a cake. →*
***Feeling hungry**, he bought a cake.* (cause)

Participles can be used after many conjunctions, for example—*as, after, before, since, when, once, without, in spite of.*

***Before leaving**, he gave me a present.*
*He swam **in spite of having** a sore arm.*

Having + past participle is a special form that shows the cause of a second action or a sequence of actions.

***After running the marathon**, he was exhausted. →*
***Having run the marathon**, he was exhausted.*

Gerunds can function as the subject of the sentence.

***Talking** is the best therapy.*

The subject of the participial phrase is usually the same as the subject in the main clause.

Running around until they were tired, the kids had fun. (the kids ran and the kids had fun)

NOT: *~~Waiting for hours, the day seemed to Tom as if it would never end.~~ (Tom was waiting; the day wasn't)*

Unit Vocabulary

<u>Books</u>

I couldn't put it down
It's very readable
It's a page-turner
based on a true story
It was very moving/gripping
the characters are one-dimensional
a bookworm
an avid reader
a best-seller
hooked
depict

<u>Compound adjectives</u>

single-minded
kind-hearted
level-headed
self-sufficient
stand-offish
absent-minded
thick-skinned
career-oriented

<u>Humor</u>

a farce
a pun
cartoons
black humor
surreal humor
irony
exaggeration
satire

REFERENCE

Unit 4 Reference

Future probability

Use *will* to talk about something that is definite or a very strong probability.

Use *could*, *may*, or *might* to talk about something that is possible but not certain.

There are many other phrases for describing possibility.

Adverbs and adverbial phrases:

it will almost definitely, it almost definitely won't, it will presumably

Verb phrases:

it may well, it might well, I doubt

Adjectives and adjective phrases:

it's bound to, certain to, sure to, unlikely to

Noun phrases:

the chances are that, there's a strong/slight possibility, you don't have a hope of ___-ing

Future forms: review

For timetables:

Use the simple present to talk about timetables.

*The plane **departs** at 2:30 from Rio.*

For decisions, plans and intentions:

Use *will* to talk about a decision made at the time of speaking (including offers and promises).

***I'll have** a coffee. Thanks.*

Use *going to* to talk about a plan or intention (maybe details haven't been decided yet).

***I'm going to work** in finance.*

Use the present continuous to talk about a future arrangement (details such as time and place have been decided).

***I'm playing** tennis at 4:30 with Zara.*

For predictions:

Use *will* to make predictions based on what you know or believed. We often use words like *think*, *hope*, *believe*, with *will* in this case.

*I think Mike **will be** a good manager.*

Use *going to* to make predictions based on what you can see, hear, think, or feel now.

*I think **I'm going to** be sick.*

Use the future continuous to talk about something that will be in progress at a definite time in the future.

*This time next year **I'll be living** in France.*

Use the future continuous to ask about someone's plans.

***Will** you **be working** late tonight?*

Use the future perfect with time phrases with *by*, for example—*by that time, by this time next week, by the end of February, by the end of the day*, etc.

***By** June we **will have finished** the project.*

Subject/verb inversion

We use inversion to emphasize the adverbial phrase in a sentence. Inversion is usually used in more formal writing.

Form: negative or adverbial expression + auxiliary verb + subject. Note: the word order is the same as the question form.

***Not once did she** look up from her book.*

Do not use auxiliary verbs when the main verb is the verb *be* or a modal verb.

***Not only is he** a great musician, but he can also teach.*

Inversion can be used after restrictive words; for example—*never, rarely, little, hardly.*

***Never before had he** seen such a beautiful vase.*

Inversion is also used with phrases beginning with *only*. These emphasize the first clause.

***Only** when I heard her speak **did I** remember her.*

Use *no way* + inversion to show that something is impossible or that the speaker doesn't want to do something. It is informal.

***No way would I** do a bungee jump!*

Unit Vocabulary

Progress

genetic engineering, virus, space mission, antibiotics

Arrangements

get out of, lined up, tied up, be free, fall through, be up to, call off, be on, wind down, swamped, come up

Special abilities

gifted, adulation, a freak, in the making, peers, a prodigy, demanding

Unit 5 Reference

Emphasis

Passive constructions can be used to emphasize information at the beginning of a sentence.

*The suspect **was arrested** by police.*

Fronting

The order of clauses in a sentence can be changed to put a clause at the beginning that would not normally be there.

***What she thinks she is doing,** I don't know!*

Cleft sentences

Clauses beginning with *It is*, *It was*, or *What* can be used for emphasis.

***It was Ellen** who spotted the mistake.*

Adding words for emphasis

*She used her **own** ingredients.*

*They aren't **the least bit** scared.*

*I haven't thought about it **at all**.*

*Some people were **even** asking for discounts.*

*I **do** think we should warn them about the delay.*

Conditionals: review

To talk about something that is always true, use *if* + simple present in the *if* clause, and the simple present in the result clause.

***If** you **go** into business with relatives, it **tends** to put a strain on your relationship.*

To talk about a possible real situation in the future, use *if* + present tense in the *if* clause, and *will* (*might, may, could, should*) in the result clause.

***If** we **find** a bank, we **could change** some money.*

To talk about a hypothetical or unlikely situation in the future, use *if* + simple past in the *if* clause, and *would* (*might, may, could, should*) in the result clause.

***If** they **asked** me to go back, I **wouldn't hesitate**.*

To talk about a hypothetical past situation, use *if* + past perfect in the *if* clause, and *would have* (*could have, should have, might have*) in the result clause.

***If** he **had taken** his phone, I **could've called** him.*

To talk about past regrets, use *if only* or *I wish* + past perfect.

***If only** I **hadn't told** him about Johnny.*

***I wish** I'**d thought** of looking it up on the Internet—it **would've saved** so much time.*

Mixed conditionals

These may express a hypothetical present result of a past action: *if* + past perfect in the *if* clause, and *would, could, may, might*, or *should* in the result clause.

***If** we **hadn't answered** the advertisement, we **wouldn't** be here now.*

Other words and phrases can be used with, or instead of, *if* in conditional sentences, for example—*provided that, as long as, if only, should you happen to, supposing, if it hadn't been for*

Sentence adverbials

Sentence adverbials are adverbial phrases that modify part of a sentence. They can be used to show the speaker's attitude toward a subject, to organize information, rephrase, change the subject, summarize or generalize, etc. They are usually separated from the rest of the sentence by a comma.

***Broadly speaking**, we all agree.*

Common adverbials: *fundamentally, essentially, broadly speaking, however, surprisingly enough, seemingly, apparently, up to a point, on the other hand, looking back, in hindsight, believe it or not*

Unit Vocabulary

Money, achievement, and charity

come into a fortune	high-income	haggle
stock market	go bankrupt	a raise
paid on commission	priceless	sue
philanthropist	volunteer	vision
power of attorney	provide for	
business venture	not see a penny	
declare bankruptcy	put money into research	

Expressing priorities

the essential thing	vital
couldn't do without	my first priority
not concerned about something	

Describing a job

freedom/autonomy	401K
convenient location	salary
working environment	benefits
flexible working hours	job satisfaction
opportunity for promotion	challenging work
professional development	
supportive colleagues/manager	

Speaking Exchange

Unit 1 | Page 14, Exercise 2a

Carlos Acosta
An Artistic Superstar

Carlos Acosta is the greatest ballet dancer of his generation—a man sometimes called "Air Acosta" for his incredible jumps and leaps—and he has been setting the classical dance world on fire for over a decade and a half.

Born in 1973 in Cuba, Acosta was one of 11 children. He lived with his family in a cramped one-bedroom apartment in Havana, where he dreamed of one day being a soccer star. Acosta's childhood was one of poverty, brushes with crime, and frequent absences from school. Fearing that his son was becoming a delinquent, Acosta's strong-willed father enrolled him in ballet school at age 9. Pedro Acosta was determined that his son would escape from the poverty in which they lived.

Much, if not all of the credit for Acosta's start as a dancer goes to his father. When Acosta was expelled from his first ballet school for absences, his father went to the school and arranged a transfer. He continued to push his son, despite the fact that Carlos did not at first like ballet and endured much teasing and fighting for being a boy ballet dancer. Despite his mixed feelings about ballet, Carlos eventually trained at the National Ballet School of Cuba. His hard work paid off, and in January 1990 Acosta won the Gold Medal at the Prix de Lausanne. In November of the same year he won the Grand Prix and Gold Medal at the Paris ballet competition.

It was upon winning the Prix de Lausanne, his first competition, that Acosta realized that his talent was world-class. He was the last competitor to perform, and had entered the competition at the last minute. "My greatest hope was to reach the final," he says. "I never dreamed of winning." Of all the awards he has won, Acosta says that the Prix de Lausanne means the most to him.

After winning the Prix de Lausanne, Acosta spent a year in Turin, Italy, and then joined the English National Ballet. He returned to join the National Ballet of Cuba in 1992. After that, he danced with the Houston Ballet, and finally the Royal Ballet in England, where he has been the principal guest artist since 2003.

Acosta has performed the principal male role in nearly every classical ballet. He holds dual Cuban and British citizenship. Yet he still feels like an exile and misses his homeland. The title of his 2007 autobiography is *No Way Home*. It is ironic that, though Acosta's father is responsible for forcing his son to begin ballet, it is ballet that has caused Acosta to build a life apart from his family. "I didn't choose ballet, and for years I rebelled against it, believing it kept me from my family, from home, and from happiness," he says. "But I have come to terms with it. It has taken many years."

Though he is still a commanding force on the stage, Acosta is looking ahead to a time when he will retire from ballet. "You can only go on so long," he says. "I have done all the repertoire, all the Swan Lakes. If you are an artist and you want to keep seeking and growing and discovering things, you could get to a dead end, if you know what I mean." So what will be next for Acosta? For a start, he has begun experimenting with modern dance, including a collaboration with contemporary choreographer Russell Maliphant. "I'm searching for a transition," Acosta says. "The artistry is still in me. It's a question of finding the right vocabulary and language for your artistry." And for Acosta, that means moving into contemporary dance.

And his ultimate ambition? To return to Cuba, where he has bought a large house, and to create a new dance company there. "I would like to create a bridge from Cuba to the world, so that all the choreographers like Russell Maliphant can come and maybe try different things with the dancers there." In the meantime, Acosta continues to dazzle audiences around the world with his incandescent performances.

Unit 3 | Page 40, Exercise 10a

Student B

The queen is traveling through the countryside when she decides that she wants to drive. The chauffeur gets into the back of the car, and the queen gets into the front and starts driving. She goes too fast, and a police officer stops the car. One minute later the police officer calls headquarters.

"I can't make an arrest," he says. "This person is too important."

"Who is it?" asks the police chief. "The mayor?"

"No. Someone even more important than that."

"The governor?"

"No. Someone even more important than that."

"The president?"

"No. Someone even more important than that."

"Who can possibly be more important than the president?" asks the chief.

"I don't know, chief, but he has the queen as his chauffeur."

Unit 5 | Page 66, Exercise 8

Group B

You are the managers. You want:

- to build a new cafeteria with better food. The workers want a gym and swimming pool. You think the cafeteria is more important. You can't build both.
- to arrange buses for employees to come to work, but the employees must pay for a portion of the fare.
- to install some modern art in the reception area. This is to impress clients who visit the office.

Which issues are very important, important, not so important?

Decide how you will negotiate for what you want.

Unit 4 | Page 52, Exercise 7a

Text A

Not only _______ (1.) Junichi Ono have his first exhibition when he was eight, but the young artist _______ (2.) met Junichiro Koizumi and George W. Bush, such was his fame as a young prodigy. The boy had always been artistic. Only _______ (3.) he drew his first character, "Liberty-kun," at the age of six, _______ (4.) his mother, a designer, realize he was truly gifted. The picture, based on the Statue of Liberty, made Ono famous as a Japanese pop artist. Rarely _______ (5.) a day go by when Junichi isn't producing at least one new work. _______ (6.) occasionally do people notice how different he is. "He's a little strange," says one student. "He talks to himself a lot," says another.

Unit 5 | Page 66, Exercise 8

Group A

You are the employees. You want:

- to build a gym and a swimming pool for employees to use at lunch and after work.
- free buses to and from work.
- overtime pay.
- to update the kitchen equipment.

Which issues are very important, important, not so important?

Decide how you will negotiate for what you want.

Unit 3 | Page 40, Exercise 10a

Student A

An artist has been displaying his paintings in an art gallery. He asks the gallery owner if anyone has bought his work.

"I have good news and bad news," says the gallery owner. "The good news is that a man asked if your work would be worth more after your death. I told him it would, and he bought all ten of your paintings."

"That's wonderful," says the artist. "What's the bad news?"

"The man was your doctor."

Unit 4 | Page 52, Exercise 7a

Text B

Not _____ (1.) is Abigail Sin one of Singapore's greatest pianists; she is _____ (2.) a gifted mathematician, and she was able to read at the age of two. No sooner _____ (3.) Abigail Sin taken her first piano lesson at the age of five than she became hooked on the instrument. Only _____ (4.) she has completely mastered a piece of music _____ (5.) she stop for a break, sometimes practicing for 30 hours a week. Her twin brother, Josiah, is also talented, but the difference is the "fire inside." "She always practices the same stuff over and over again," complains the ten-year-old boy. _____ (6.) way would average children have the dedication to practice like this. While they are out playing with their friends, Abigail can be found in the music room, hammering away at the keys.

Unit 5 | Page 59, Exercise, 2a

Reading B

RICHES TO RAGS

Most people who dream of winning the lottery assume that a big win would mean the end to all of their financial problems. Sometimes, however, winning a lot of money brings on an entirely new set of problems. Take, for example, William "Bud" Post, who won $16.2 million in the Pennsylvania lottery but ended up with nothing. "Everybody dreams of winning money, but nobody realizes the nightmares that come out of the woodwork, or the problems," he said just five years after winning. "I wish it'd never happened. It was a total nightmare."

Post's problems were partly of his own making and partly the result of friends and family who took advantage of him. "Promises he made to family members and his inability to control his spending led to most of the money he had won being squandered," said a lawyer who worked for Post. Post admitted that he went wild after his win. He bought expensive cars, motorcycles, houses, a sailboat, and a twin-engine plane. He even bought a car dealership for his brother and invested in a restaurant for another brother and sister. Neither business venture made any money for Post. Yet another of Post's brothers tried to hire a hit man to kill Post and his wife. The brother hoped to inherit Post's money.

Post had legal troubles, as well. A former girlfriend sued him for a share of the winnings, claiming that they had purchased the winning lottery ticket together. The court awarded her $5.3 million. In addition, Post served time in jail for firing a gun over the head of a bill collector. Within three months of receiving his first lottery payment, Post was $500,000 in debt. By the early 1990s, he had declared bankruptcy.

Post spent the last years of his life living quietly on a $450 monthly Social Security check. Once the money was gone, he was more content. "That's all I want. Just peace of mind," he declared.

Unit 3 | Page 40, Exercise 10a

Student C

A woman goes to a doctor, complaining of pain.
"Where does it hurt?" asks the doctor.
"Everywhere," says the woman.
"Can you be more specific?"
So the woman touches her knee with her finger. "Ow!" she says. Then she touches her nose. "Ow!" Then she touches her back. "Ow!" Finally, she touches her cheek. "Ow!"
The doctor tells her to sit down, takes one look at her and says, "You have a broken finger."

Writing Bank

Unit 2 | Page 25, Exercise 11

Formal emails

1 Read the email and answer the questions.

1. What did Mr. Reiss want?
2. What is Ms. Du Pont offering?
3. What can't she give Mr. Reiss?
4. What can't she go to?

funding for Reiss Co—Inbox

delete | junk | reply | reply all | forward | print

To: breiss@medal.com
From: mdupont@pringle.com
Subject: Funding for Reiss Co.

Dear Mr. Reiss,

Regarding your request for funding for your website, I am pleased to inform you that we are able to offer you an investment of $5,000. This will be a one-time contribution and will not be renewable. However, we do review our investments annually and may decide to make further contributions in subsequent years. I am afraid that due to company policy, we are unable to offer a monthly payment.

Finally, I would like to thank you for the invitation to the launch party. Unfortunately, I have a prior engagement and will be unable to attend.

Best of luck with your new venture. I look forward to hearing from you soon.

Regards,

Marissa Du Pont

Writing skill | redrafting

2 After writing an email, you need to check it at least twice. Below are five things to check for. Match them to the examples of mistakes below.

____ 1. greeting and signing off appropriately
____ 2. coherence and cohesion
____ 3. punctuation—do not write in capital letters or use multiple exclamations
____ 4. spelling or typing mistakes
____ 5. formal style

a. Manny thanks, We have recieved the shipment.

b. We are ABSOLUTELY DELIGHTED that Holborn Company has been able to guarantee the deal!!

c. Dear Mrs. Winston,
Thanks for the invitation, but I can't really go to the event because I've got tons of work to do right now.

d. I have a number of questions concerning the contract. It is an excellent job opportunity. The salary is lower than I had expected. It also proposes that I work abroad for one month per year. It may pose a problem.

e. Hi Mr. Kawazaka,
Regarding your email on January 15th, 2007 . . .

Useful Phrases

Apologizing	• *I would like to apologize for the delay.*
Giving good or bad news	• *I am pleased to inform you that . . .* • *I regret to inform you that . . .*
Making a request	• *We would be grateful if you could . . .*
Responding to a request	• *We would be happy to . . .* • *I am afraid we are unable to . . .*
Complaining	• *I am writing to complain about . . .*
Responding to an invitation	• *We would be very happy to come to . . .* • *I am afraid I will be unable to attend.*

Phrasal Verbs

A phrasal verb consists of two or more words: a verb + a particle (an adverb or a preposition) [+ a preposition]. The meaning of a phrasal verb is usually very different from the meaning of the verb alone. For example, the phrasal verbs *look up* (search for in a book or other source) and *look after* (care for) have very different meanings from *look*.

Some phrasal verbs are intransitive, (they cannot take an object). The majority are transitive (they take an object). Sometimes the object can come after the particle or after the verb. For example, hand in your papers / hand your papers in / hand them in. These phrasal verbs are known as *separable*. With other phrasal verbs the words in the phrase cannot be separated; they are known as *inseparable*.

Some common phrasal verbs

Separable	
Ask out	ask someone on a date
Bring up	1) raise children 2) mention a subject
Call back	return a phone call
Call off	cancel
Call up	make a phone call
Figure out	find the solution
Fill in	give detailed information
Fill out	writing information on a form
Fill up	fill completely
Give back	return
Hand out	give to each person in a group; distribute
Hold up	keep waiting
Look over	examine carefully
Look up	search for information in a book or other source
Make up	Invent (a story)
Pick up	1) lift 2) collect in a car
Put away	put something where it belongs
Put back	return to the place it was found
Put off	Delay doing something you don't want to do; procrastinate
Shut off	turn off; stop
Show up	make someone feel stupid or bad
Split up	to end a relationship
Take back	return
Tear down	destroy
Try on	put something on to check the fit
Turn around	change direction
Turn down	refuse
Turn in	1) produce a great result 2) tell the police about a criminal 3) go to bed
Turn up	increase the volume
Work out	resolve a problem

Inseparable	
Catch on	1) understand 2) become popular
Come across	find by chance
Come by	visit
Come from	born in a place; originate
Come up with	invent or create something
Cut back/down on	use less; reduce
Fit in	be accepted by others
Get along with	have a friendly relationship
Get away from	escape
Get away with	go unnoticed or unpunished
Get in	enter
Get over	recover
Get up	get out of bed
Give up	stop trying
Go on	1) continue 2) happen
Go for	choose
Go through	1) experience 2) spend 3) check 4) be approved
Grow up	become an adult
Hang up	end a phone conversation
Keep out of	stay away from; not be involved
Make off with	steal
Make up	apologize after a quarrel
Look into	investigate
Look forward to	anticipate
Look up to	admire
Put up with	tolerate
See to	deal with someone or something
Take after	look or behave like a relative
Turn up	appear suddenly
Work out	exercise

Audioscript

UNIT 1 Achieving goals

1.02 (Page 9)

A: Mark, you speak seven languages.

B: That's right.

A: Can you tell us a little about your level of fluency and proficiency in the languages?

B: Well, Russian is probably my best language. I speak it pretty well because I spent a lot of time there, but it's a little rusty. I have a good ear, which is a good thing and a bad thing, because my accent makes people think that I know more than I really do. The other languages are mainly Latin-based: Spanish, Portuguese, Italian, but also French and Polish.

A: You learned the languages through a combination of techniques.

B: That's right: classes, travel, private study . . .

A: Did you use any special techniques? Any magic secrets?

B: Magic secrets, no. But I did do some interesting things, like memory training. I watched movies in their original languages, and at some point I tried sticking lists of words around the house. But I think for me it was more a case of being motivated. My biggest motivator was a love of languages and pleasure in communicating with people from other countries.

A: Would you say it's easier to learn new languages if you already know languages in that family? For example, you speak Spanish and French, so was it easy to pick up Portuguese?

B: I wouldn't say it was easy, but yeah, I would definitely say it helps. Occasionally it gets confusing, though. You might be speaking in one language and suddenly a word from another language slips out, causing complete confusion.

A: Is there any little word of encouragement you could offer those poor souls who are trying to master a language?

B: Hmm . . . that's a tricky one. What I would say is that knowing how to read and write a language doesn't mean you can speak it. You really have to get out there and try to speak at every opportunity. Take risks. Don't be afraid to look stupid, because that's the only way you're going to learn. And everyone has to start somewhere. When I was young, I went to France, after years of studying French, and, to my complete embarrassment, I couldn't speak the language or understand anything. All I could do was order breakfast in my hotel!

1.03 (Page 12)

To continue our series on famous firsts . . .

If you ask a Brazilian who first flew an airplane, she'll tell you it was Alberto Santos Dumont. Ask an American, and he'll answer the Wright brothers. In 1906, Santos Dumont was widely believed to have flown the first plane that was heavier than air. Others say that the Americans Wilbur and Orville Wright first flew in 1903. The truth is, we don't really know who flew first, though Santos Dumont was certainly a colorful character. He's said to be the first person to have owned a flying machine for personal use. He kept his balloon tied up outside his Paris apartment and regularly flew to restaurants!

Question 2 . . . It's commonly assumed that Alexander Graham Bell invented the telephone, but now we're not so sure. Many people believe that Antonio Meucci, an Italian immigrant, got there first. And in 2003, files were discovered which suggest that a twenty-six-year-old German science teacher, Philipp Reis, invented the phone fifteen years before Bell.

Now, who was the first to the North Pole? In 1908, Dr. Frederick Cook said he'd done it, but it's commonly believed that he lied, and that a man named Robert Peary made it first. There are others who claim that neither of them reached the North Pole.

The light bulb. It's widely assumed that Thomas Edison invented it, but we don't really know for sure. Edison based a lot of his inventions on other people's ideas. Also, he worked with a team, and he never shared the credit.

Moving on to our soccer question, it's widely assumed that South America's soccer glory belongs to Brazil and Argentina. But it was Uruguay that hosted and won the first World Cup in 1930. They beat Argentina 4–2 in the final, in front of 93,000 people in Montevideo. The cheering of the crowd is said to have been the loudest noise ever heard in Uruguay.

Speaking of sports, it is often thought that rugby and sheep are the main claims to fame for New Zealand. Not many people know that in 1893 New Zealand became the first country to allow women to vote.

OK, question 7: Ellen MacArthur is sometimes wrongly assumed to be the first woman to sail around the world. She wasn't. She was the fastest but not the first. That honor goes to Naomi James, who did it in 1979. Apparently, she got so seasick that soon afterward she gave up sailing altogether.

And our final question. The ancient Olympic Games were of course first held in Greece. They were very different from the Games today. Instead of medals, the winners received a crown of laurel leaves. They were also said to be allowed to put their statue up on Olympus.

1.04 (Page 13)

In the news today . . .

A conservation institute has produced kittens by cross-breeding cloned adult wild cats. It is believed to be the first time that clones of wild animals have been bred. Researchers at the Audubon Center for Research of Endangered Species say that the development holds enormous potential for the preservation of endangered species.

Australian teenager Jessica Watson has succeeded in her attempt to become the youngest person to sail solo around the world. The 16-year old battled raging storms and monster 40-foot waves during her 7-month journey. In an interview following her triumphant arrival in Sydney Harbor, Ms. Watson stressed that teenagers, girls in particular, can do so much more than people generally expect of them.

And finally, the story of a man who has entered the record books as the world's most renowned eater of burgers. It is estimated that Don Gorske has eaten over 15,000 Big Macs, and he even proposed to his girlfriend Mary in the parking lot of a McDonald's. In fifteen years, he says, he has missed a Big Mac on only seven occasions, including the death of his mother, a snowstorm and a 600-mile drive without a McDonald's in sight.

1.05 (Page 16)

1. When I was in college, a friend of mine was injured in an accident while playing football. He was paralyzed and needed to spend the rest of his life in a wheelchair. Together with some friends I decided to organize a sponsored bike ride to raise money for his family and other people in similar situations. So we set up a charity called "One Step Ahead" and arranged to bike from Scotland to Gibraltar. I'd never done anything like that before, so it was a fantastic learning experience. I'd always thought it would be great to bike across a whole country, but this exceeded my expectations. There were about twenty or thirty of us on bikes, and the rest of the crew in vans with all the equipment and camping gear. It was very tough, especially in Spain where we had to battle against the heat. But we had a fantastic time, and at the end, when we arrived, there was a huge party. We were even on the news! We felt we'd accomplished something really important, and most importantly, we raised lots of money for people with spinal injuries.
2. I've been doing volunteer work here in the rain forest, in Brazil, for a while now. Next week I'll have been here for three months, helping to teach English to the young children in the village. It's been an amazing experience. I'd never even left the U.S. before, so you can imagine how different things are for me here. When I arrived I really didn't know what to expect. It was a real culture shock, and I was here on my own for the first couple of months. Now my girlfriend has joined me, and things are a little bit easier. I've been living with a small tribe of people in the forest. I'd never done any teaching before, so the whole thing has been quite a challenge, and I've learned a lot. But some of the children are speaking pretty good English with me now, and a few of them are actually starting to write little stories, so I feel a real sense of achievement.
3. I ran the Cracovia Marathon last year. It was my first marathon, and it was great. It felt like a major achievement. I had to train really hard, getting up early in the morning to run before going to work. And as the distances got longer I had to get up earlier and earlier. It was incredibly hard, because I'd never done any training like that before. I've always run, just for myself, to relax and keep fit, but this was a chance to be more competitive and really push myself to the limit. It was a fantastic run, because Cracovia is a beautiful city, and there's such a special atmosphere as you go

along the route, with people cheering you on. My parents even came over from Australia to see me cross the finish line. I couldn't move for about a week afterwards, but I was glad I'd done it, and I'm looking forward to the next one.

1.06 (Page 16)

1. Jake, this is my friend Amy, whom I've known forever.
2. I asked what had happened, but nobody could tell me.
3. I chose this school because I'd heard it was the best.
4. Before I came to the U.S., I'd never been abroad.
5. I'm so exhausted. I've been working really hard.
6. By the time she retires, she'll have been working there for more than fifty years.

1.07 (Page 18)

If you chose mostly (a), then you are very comfortable as you are, and you're not too interested in new challenges. I think you need to make an effort to get off the couch. Go on! Take a risk—it might have a positive effect!

Now, if your answers were mainly (b), it means you love a challenge and you take advantage of your opportunities. You're willing to try anything and everything. So, good luck, but be careful!

Those of you who chose mainly (c), well, you tend to check everything out before committing yourself. You are very cautious. You may live a long, safe life, but a bit of a challenge from time to time won't do you any harm!

UNIT 2 Places and communities

1.08 (Page 20)

1. I'm from South Africa. I spent two and a half years, actually more like two years, living in Vancouver, Canada. My wife and I were trying to set up our own business there as packagers in the publishing industry. Unfortunately, things weren't going very well economically. Canada wasn't in a depression, but it wasn't a very good time to try and start your own business in publishing. What did I like about Vancouver? Well, Vancouver is one of the most beautiful cities in the world. In fact, Vancouver is regularly named as one of the best places in the world to live. It's stunningly beautiful, with mountains, sea, forests and natural beauty. Vancouver is a city where you can walk to the beach on your lunch break if you want to. You can take a bus and go skiing in the mountains forty minutes later. Canadian food is not at the top of the world's list of good food, but Vancouver has very large Chinese and Indian populations, as well as people from all over the world, so you can eat some very good food in Vancouver. The only food that people might consider uniquely Vancouverite is what they would call "fusion" cuisine, which mixes Asian, European, and local cuisines. My best memories about Canada? Well, the open spaces, the vastness, and the friendly people.
2. I'm from Mexico originally, but over the past ten years I've lived in Spain, Austria, France, and other parts of the UK. I lived in Austria for a year when I was about twenty-two. I was studying German, so I wanted to spend a year in a German-speaking country. I was a teaching assistant. I worked in a school four days a week, which meant I had long weekends. I usually traveled with my friends on the weekends. We went to Slovenia, The Czech Republic, Italy, and Germany. Some other great things about living there were skiing and ice skating on lakes. The scenery was spectacular, and the people were really welcoming. The thing I didn't really like was the food, because I'm vegetarian, and in Austria they eat a lot of meat. Apart from that, everything else was great. I think my favorite memories of Austria are the scenery, being able to go off into the mountains after school every afternoon, and going skiing or swimming in the lakes in the summer. I'd definitely like to go back one day.
3. I lived in Japan, actually in Tokyo, for about two years. It was, as you can imagine, a completely crazy experience for me, coming from my small, quiet home town. I was living in Tokyo because I was working as an English language teacher for a language school in a suburb of Tokyo. I really loved Tokyo. It was such an interesting experience. It was like being dropped into a lifestyle that was completely different from my own. Even going to the supermarket was an adventure, because I couldn't read anything. I got a few surprises, a few foods that I'd never seen before, but they were usually good. I think my favorite memories of the country would have to be the people. Because I was teaching English, I knew a lot of Japanese people as students and as colleagues in the school. They were friendly, funny, and really interested in what a foreigner like me was doing in Tokyo. They were very helpful when it came to explaining things like social customs in Japan. It was a really rewarding experience, some of the best times of my life.

1.09 (Page 23)

A: The Internet has made a big difference in my life. I mean, communication is so much easier than it was before.

B: Sure, I'd agree with that. But I still say that face-to-face communication is better. Sending an email is not nearly as personal and meaningful as a conversation.

A: Well, it depends . . .

B: On what?

A: Well, an email isn't as good as seeing someone you love, or your friends, but I'd much rather email my clients then go to meetings or talk on the phone. It saves time.

B: True, but I just think the more we use email, the more we need it. It's like an addiction, with people checking their emails every five minutes, even in meetings.

A: Yeah, but I'd still rather have it than not.

B: And, there's so much false information. Do you use it to do research?

A: All the time. I think it's OK. Maybe it's not quite as good as looking in books. It's not as reliable, but it's considerably faster.

B: I'd say that looking something up on the Internet is only slightly less reliable than shouting out the window, "Does anybody know the answer to this?" It's not regulated. Anyone can publish anything on the Internet, and it may or may not be true.

A: Well the best thing about the Internet is that it lets you do things more cheaply than before, like buying plane tickets, and buying stuff on e-bay.

B: I've never used e-bay.

A: Or Amazon. You love buying books . . .

B: Yeah, but I'd rather go to a second hand bookstore. I'm not into the idea of giving my credit card information over the Internet. No way.

A: There're lots of security measures these days . . .

1.10 (Page 30)

1. I'm a member of an alumni club, which is basically a way to keep in touch with your old friends from school. Every five or ten years we have a reunion and remember the old days, some good, some bad . . . We also get involved in some charity events. Recently, we actually sponsored some events to save our old school, which was going to be closed. I felt really great about that. We meet only once every two years as a group. We have a big party and reunite with all the people that we remember, and some of the teachers as well. What's really interesting about the group is that we've all known each other now for about 20 years. It's so interesting to meet people every two years and see how they've changed. I'm sure that if I hadn't seen those people for 20 years, I wouldn't recognize them on the street now. Hmm . . . if there's something that I don't like, it's that it's very difficult to keep in touch when you only meet every two years. And sometimes people aren't as involved as they should be, sometimes you don't hear anything for a year or two. But I will definitely stick with it, because it keeps me better connected than I probably would be if I weren't a member.
2. I'm a member of a ballroom dancing club. There are lessons, but it's also social. There's about . . . oh I suppose . . . it must be about thirty people in the club, and I think I'm the youngest there. I go with a friend of mine, who's my dance partner. It's really fun. I joined about six months ago on a whim because I just had an urge to try ballroom dancing. I've never been very coordinated as a dancer, and I'm not very good at choreography, but it's been really great. There are a lot of beginners in the class, so I never feel out of place. We meet once a week, in a local school gym. We meet in the evenings after work, and it can be hard to get out of

the house in the evening, but it's so much fun, it's well worth the effort. So far we've been learning . . . the Waltz, the Foxtrot, and some Latin dances like the Jive and the Tango. I love it.

UNIT 3 Stories

1.11 (Page 33)

1. In 1957 a news program called *Panorama* broadcast a story about spaghetti trees in Switzerland. While the reporter told the story, Swiss farmers in the background were picking spaghetti from trees. Following this, thousands of people called the show, asking how to grow spaghetti trees.
2. In 1998 large numbers of Americans went to Burger King asking for a new type of burger. The food company had published an ad in USA Today announcing the new "left-handed Whopper," a burger designed for left-handed people. The following day, Burger King admitted that they had been joking all along.

1.12 (Page 35)

1. My favorite fictional character is Linda Hammerick, in the book *Bitter in the Mouth*, by Monique Truong. Linda, or Lin Dao, as we later learn is her real name, is a really strong-minded girl growing up in North Carolina, in the U.S. The story is partly about her difficult relationship with her mother and grandmother, and partly about the problems that Linda has to overcome. She has a condition known as synesthesia, which in her case means that almost every word triggers an actual taste in her mouth. For example, every time she hears her own name, Linda, she tastes mint. Every time she hears the word *you*, she tastes canned green beans, and so on. The thing is, it's not until the end of the book that she learns that this is a condition that other people have, that she's not alone. So she spends the first 30 years of her life trying to hide what's going on from everyone except Kelly, her best friend. (The name Kelly tastes like canned peaches, by the way.) One of the other really interesting things about the character is we don't learn until halfway through the book that she's Vietnamese American. So, even though the book describes her as having long, dark hair, the picture I had in my mind changed slightly halfway through the book. I thought that was kind of cool. Anyway, I admire Linda for her strength, and also for her ability to empathize with others, to see things from their perspective.
2. I think my favorite fictional character has to be the lead character, the heroine of Jane Austen's *Pride and Prejudice*. I think she's one of the best-drawn characters in literature. She is of course Elizabeth Bennett. She's lively, she's feisty, and when you think that this is a book that's set in the 1800s, it's really remarkable that such a modern woman is the heroine. I mean, she talks back to all these men who are older than her and in more authority than her. It's great. She's a good role model for today's women too. I imagine her as being pretty tall, with a lively face and dark hair. Hmm . . . memorable things that she does: well, the thing that I really like about her is the way that she takes control of her own life in a period of history when women really had very little power and very little control over who they married. She sort of comes to a self-realization through the events of the novel and decides to go for the guy that she really loves. She has problems along the way: people who think she's socially unacceptable, or people who have very typical views about class and society. But, of course, she succeeds and wins Mr. Darcy, her true love, in the end.
3. I think my favorite fictional character is the old man from *The Old Man and the Sea*, by Ernest Hemingway. I still have a strong visual image of this man. The whole story takes place in a boat off the coast of Cuba, with just this one character, mostly. I imagine him to be pretty old. He was a lifelong fisherman. He had a tough life, so I imagine he had really big strong hands that were . . . cut and bruised from hauling in nets every night out in the ocean. I imagine him with a little bit of grey hair, old and wise, somebody who took a lot of pride in his work. He is down on his luck in the story. He hasn't caught anything for a long time, but he still drags himself out every night and casts his nets and hopes that he'll catch something.

   In a way, he sort of reminds me of my father, somebody who had limited opportunities in life, but found a job that he could do and did it to the best of his ability.

1.13 (Page 39)

Groucho Marx didn't want to be a comedian at first. He loved reading and singing, and he wanted to become a doctor. But his mother had other ideas. She persuaded Groucho and his brothers to start a group called The Six Mascots. During a radio show they started making jokes, and that's when they decided to become a comedy act. Their popularity grew quickly. But in 1926 the boys' mother died, and the Great Depression began. In the 1930's a man called Irving Thalberg helped the Marx Brothers to get on television. They made their most famous movies, the last of which was called *A Day At the Races*. After this, Groucho became a radio host and he also made more movies, but without his brothers. In the 1970's he toured with a live one-man show, but by now in his nineties he was getting weaker, and he died in 1977.

1.14 (Page 40)

Three colleagues, a photographer, a journalist and an editor are covering a political convention. One day, during their lunch break, they walk along a beach, and one of them sees a lamp. He picks it up and rubs it, and a magic genie suddenly appears. The genie says "You can each have one wish." So the photographer says, "I want to spend the rest of my life in a big house in the mountains with a beautiful view, where I can take photographs." Poof! Suddenly the photographer is gone to his home in the mountains. Then it's the journalist's turn. "I want to live in a big house in the countryside with an enormous garden where I can sit and write for the rest of my life." Poof! The journalist is gone. Finally, the genie says to the editor, "And what about you? What's your wish?" So the editor says, "I want those two back before lunch. We've got a deadline at 6:00 tonight."

UNIT 4 Moving forward

1.15 (Page 43)

Resistance to antibiotics is on the increase. Research out today shows an increase in the number and strength of superbugs, resistant to normal antibiotics. Analysis of particularly resistant strains, kept in laboratory test tubes, shows that in the last twelve months . . .

A new virus, developed by hackers in South East Asia has been crashing computer networks around the globe. The virus penetrates standard firewalls to affect computer software and eventually data stored in the microchip. Experts have warned that . . .

A breakthrough in genetic engineering technology means that human cloning can now enable scientists to re-build damaged organs in children. Cells taken from skin tissue are used to provide the necessary genes, which are then implanted . . .

The ongoing budget crisis has been cited as the reason for the latest delay to the space mission. The new shuttle, Discover XVIII, which was originally due to launch last Thursday, is set to orbit Mars, scanning the surface for evidence of early life-forms.

1.16 (Page 44)

A: It says name four superheroes. Can you think of any?
B: Well, there's . . . let's see . . . Superman . . .
C: Spiderman, Batman . . .
B: The Incredible Hulk . . .
C: The Fantastic Four . . .
B: The Incredibles . . .
A: Well, that's definitely more than four . . . Should we move on? The next one is about the color of the Incredible Hulk . . .
C: He was green, wasn't he?
B: I heard the original comic book version was actually grey, but a printing error made him appear green, and the comic's writers decided that it suited him, so they let it stay.
A: Oh . . . what do you know? OK—can you name four of Spiderman's special powers?
B: Well, he can walk up walls using his spider-grip, he has super-strength . . .
C: . . . and can lift up to 10 tons . . .
B: He has web shooters which he can fire to catch villains and . . . he has spider-sense . . .
C: Yes . . . a kind of ESP that allows Parker to sense when danger is afoot, and spider-speed, so he can run fast to escape danger.
A: OK . . . the name of the planet where Superman was born was . . .

C: . . . Planet Krypton, wasn't it?
A: Of course! OK, what was the name of the movie released in 2002 that broke all box office records in the first weekend?
B: Oh, that must be Spiderman, without a doubt!
A: Great! And last, the name of the female character who has super-strength, bullet-proof bracelets and . . .
C: . . . a lasso that makes people tell the truth . . . Wonder Woman!

1.17 (Page 46)

A: Legendary veteran comic writer Stan Lee co-created Spiderman and the Fantastic Four, among others.
We asked him how he thought of Spiderman, and this was his response.
B: In trying to create a superhero, the first thing you have to think of, or at least the first thing I have to think of, is a super-power. What super-power would be different, that people hadn't seen before? I had already done the Hulk, who was the strongest character on Earth; I had done a group called the Fantastic Four: one of them could fly, one was invisible, and one's body could stretch, and I was trying to think: what else can I do? And I've told this story so often that for all I know it might even be true! But I was sitting and watching a fly crawling on the wall, and I thought "Gee—that would be great—what if a character could crawl on walls like an insect?" So I had my super-power, but then I needed a name. So I thought, "Insectman" . . . that didn't sound good. Crawlingman? I went on and on . . . Mosquitoman? . . . and then somehow I said "Spiderman" and it just sounded dramatic and mysterious to me, so that was my name.
A: When asked why he made Spiderman a scientist, he replied . . .
B: I had always resented the fact that in most superhero stories and actually, in most comic books the hero is some sort of a rugged, muscular outdoorsman, a sportsman . . . an adventurer. And anybody who was literate or scholarly, they were . . . he was always considered to be somewhat of a nerd. And I thought, my gosh, people don't have enough respect for intelligence. So again, in trying to be different, and in trying to be realistic, I thought I would make my teenage hero a scholarship student, extra-bright—he was studying science. And just to show that there's no reason why a hero couldn't also be a kid who likes science and is good in school and is smart . . . and that was the thinking behind it.
A: When asked if he was at all scientific, he replied . . .
B: I'm not much of a scientist. I love reading science-fiction but when it comes to actual science, I'm . . . I'm a dummy. But I like to make things seem scientific!
A: Our final question asked if Stan Lee thought there would ever be real superheroes.
B: I believe that they will be able, through cloning . . . through genetics they will be able to find a way to abolish most diseases. They will be able . . . they will have to . . . see, once these wars are finished with, if they ever are, we're going to want to go to the planets, they're going to want to go to Mars. Now, it's such a long trip, and it'll be so hard to get back again, they're going to have to make human beings able to adapt to Mars, adapt themselves . . . or is it adopt? I never . . . I always get those two mixed up. But at any rate, I believe that they will find a way to make people able to live in the atmosphere of Mars, through altering them genetically . . . Because of genetics, I think we can do virtually anything.

1.18 (Page 48)

1. Do you think you'll still be studying English?
2. Do you think you'll have the same lifestyle?
3. Do you think you'll be living in the same place?
4. Do you think your country will have a different government?
5. Do you think you'll have changed much?
6. Do you think you'll have the same interests?
7. Do you think you'll have the same close friends?
8. Do you think you'll have seen more of the world?

1.19 (Page 49)

Conversation 1
A: Hello?
B: Hi, Kevin. It's Tina.
A: Oh hi, Tina. How are you?
B: Great. You?
A: Pretty good.
B: Are you busy this Saturday?
A: Um . . . sort of. I'm playing soccer.
B: Oh, I didn't know you played soccer.
A: I don't really. Well, once in a while.
B: Are you playing all day Saturday?
A: Yeah, pretty much all day.
B: What are you up to in the evening?
A: I might be free. Let me think. Mm, maybe about eight-ish. What are you thinking?
B: We're thinking of going to Riverside Café. . .
A: Oh yeah? I used to go there every so often when I was a student. Do you want me to pick you up?
B: Um, or should I drive?
A: I don't mind driving.
B: Actually, it'll be easier if I take my car. I think I'll drive . . .

Conversation 2
C: Lauren James.
D: Hi, sweetheart.
C: Oh, hi.
D: Still working?
C: Yep.
D: Hard day?
C: Kind of. Nothing major, just the usual.
D: Such as?
C: Filling out forms, replying to emails, that kind of thing.
D: Uh-huh.
C: Going over the schedules again, checking budgets, etcetera. Actually, there were tons of mistakes.
D: Really?
C: Yeah. But I'm almost finished.
D: Would you like me to get dinner started?
C: That would be great.
D: Pasta maybe? Or there's chicken in the fridge.
C: Chicken sounds good. I'll be home in an hour or so.
D: OK, I'll put the chicken in the oven . . . [fade out]

1.20 (Page 52)

A: Can you tell us a little bit about the case and what made it so special?
B: The case concerned a pair of twins called John and Michael. They were in their late teens, but they were very small for their age, and they wore thick glasses. They used to get laughed at in school, because, in a conventional sense, they weren't very bright or social.
A: They were outsiders.
B: Well, that's right. Outsiders. But they had an amazing gift. You could name any date in the past or future forty thousand years and they would be able to tell you what day of the week it was.
A: So I could say, for example, June 5th 1376, and they could tell me it was Sunday or Monday, etcetera?
B: That's right. But that wasn't all. During one interview, the psychologist dropped a box of matches on the floor and the twins immediately called out "one hundred and eleven." The psychologist counted the matches and there were exactly one hundred and eleven.
A: And the twins hadn't counted them?
B: No. There was no time. As soon as the matches hit the floor, they knew there were one hundred and eleven. Now another thing the twins could do was remember extremely long sequences of numbers. You could say a number of up to three hundred digits, and they were able to repeat it back to you perfectly.
A: So they basically have an extraordinary ability with numbers.
B: Not only with numbers. They have another talent, which is that you can name any day of their lives since they were about four years old, and they are able to tell you what the weather was like, what they did, and other events in the wider world. They can remember absolutely everything about that day.
A: Just any ordinary day.
B: Any and every ordinary day.
A: Obviously the twins, John and Michael, were studied at length by various psychologists, educators . . .
B: Yes, they were.
A: What progress did these people make in coming up with explanations of their ability?
B: I think the main thing is that we realize that John and Michael's ability is actually visual as well as mathematical. If you ask them how they do it, they say they can "see" the answers. When the box of matches fell, they "saw" one hundred and eleven. It wasn't a

calculation. Similarly, they can "see" themselves as five year-olds. Somehow they have an ability to record incredible numbers of things in the mind. Of course, we have no idea how it works, but it would be very interesting to learn.

1.21 (Page 54)

1. Great discoveries of our time . . . well, in the last one hundred years or so, I guess it would be medical advances, like the use of x-rays, or the discovery of penicillin by Fleming. I mean, he made that discovery almost by mistake, and it changed modern medicine completely. Or perhaps the discovery of the structure of DNA by Watson and Crick in the fifties. That paved the way for genetics and genetic engineering . . .
2. I would say that sending man to the moon was one of the greatest scientific achievements. The man who invented the liquid-fuelled rocket, Robert Goddard, was fascinated by the idea of sending a rocket into space, and he spent years researching his ideas, until he developed the first rocket, called Nell. It was 10 feet tall, and he fired it from his aunt's farm in the U.S. At first nothing happened, but when the fuel finally ignited, the rocket was launched. It only reached a disappointing 14 yards into the air though, and scientists were skeptical of its success. When the newspapers got hold of the story they wrote the headlines "Moon rocket misses target by 238,799 miles." But later, engineers in Germany and America used his ideas, and the film footage of Nell to develop military and space exploring rockets. The *New York Times* had to write Goddard a public apology.
3. Computers, definitely, especially information technology and the Internet. The whole way that information is distributed and kept has been revolutionized by information technology. And things have happened so quickly. I mean, the first computer was built in 1948, I think. And was so big it took up a whole room! If you think about the designs now, and the capacity, it's just amazing. And it has made the world a smaller place, because it is so easy now to get information about almost anything.
4. I don't think we should underestimate the importance of domestic appliances, like the washing machine, dishwasher, etcetera. These timesaving inventions made it easier for women to enter the workforce, and that has had a huge impact on society. Or maybe it should be the advances in travel, with the bicycle, then the car and the airplane. The world must have been a very different place when the fastest way to get anywhere was on a horse! . . .

UNIT 5 Making money

1.22 (Page 57)

1. He can't complain. It's his own fault he didn't get a raise.
2. We are by no means certain that it is the same man committing the crimes.
3. What I really miss is having enough time to spend with friends.
4. They didn't understand what we wanted at all.
5. The employees actually love coming to work.
6. It was always Sammy who got into trouble.
7. Keith wasn't the least bit annoyed when we cancelled the meeting.

1.23 (Page 58)

While we're on the subject of choosing business partners, I cringe whenever I hear that two old friends or family members are planning to start a business together as fifty–fifty partners. It isn't that doing business with friends and family is a bad idea—many very successful businesses are family-owned. It's just that being someone's friend or relative is one of the worst reasons I can think of for making that someone your business partner. One of the problems is that once someone becomes your business partner, there is generally only one way to get rid of them (legally, of course) if things don't work out.

You must buy them out for the fair value of their interest in the business. And that can be an expensive proposition.

There are a few ways to determine if someone has what it takes to be your business partner, however.

Firstly, you need to decide, are you a visionary, or an operations person? Successful partnerships combine those two kinds of people. A visionary is a strategic, "big picture" thinker who understands the business model, the market, and the overall business plan. An operations person is someone who rolls up their sleeves, wades up to their hip boots in the details and executes the strategy that the visionary comes up with. You are either one or the other—it is almost impossible to be both. Once you have determined if you are a "visionary" or an "operations person," look for your opposite number. That way your business is more likely to strike the right balance between strategy and tactics.

Do you have all the skills you need on board to make the business work? Perhaps you are an inventor who is excellent at product design but clueless about selling. Perhaps you have a strong marketing background but need someone to help you crunch the numbers and make sure your products or services can be delivered within budget. Your partners should complement your set of business skills, not duplicate them. Keep in mind that you can acquire someone's skills without making them a partner. If a particular skill, such as contract negotiation or bookkeeping, is not critical to the success of your business, you may be better off hiring a lawyer, accountant, or consultant to do it for you and keeping ownership of your business.

Can you communicate directly and honestly with this person, without pulling any punches? Communication between partners can often get rough; disagreements and arguments break out all the time. It is difficult to criticize someone harshly, yet sometimes you must be cruel with your business partners in order to do the right thing for your business. Your business may well suffer if you consistently hold back important information for fear of offending your partner or jeopardizing the underlying friendship or emotional bond between you.

Sometimes the most successful business partnerships are those where the partners do not socialize outside the office.

And lastly, is your business partner willing to hang around for the long haul? This is the critical test of a business partner. Many people are happy to help out with a business during its start-up phase, only to lose interest later on when something more attractive (like a job offer from a big corporation) comes along, a life-changing event (like the birth of a new child) occurs, or the going is getting tougher and the business isn't as much "fun" as it used to be. If you are not sure if someone is committed to the long-term success of your business, make them an employee or independent contractor, with perhaps an 'option' to acquire an interest in your business at a date two or three years down the road . . . provided, of course, they are still working for you at that time and you continue to be satisfied with their performance.

1.24 (Page 58)

Section 1

While we're on the subject of choosing business partners, I cringe whenever I hear that two old friends or family members are planning to start a business together as fifty–fifty partners. It isn't that doing business with friends and family is a bad idea—many very successful businesses are family-owned. It's just that being someone's friend or relative is one of the worst reasons I can think of for making that someone your business partner. One of the problems is that once someone becomes your business partner, there is generally only one way to get rid of them (legally, of course) if things don't work out.

You must buy them out for the fair value of their interest in the business. And that can be an expensive proposition.

Section 2

There are a few ways to determine if someone has what it takes to be your business partner, however.

Firstly, you need to decide, are you a visionary, or an operations person? Successful partnerships combine those two kinds of people. A visionary is a strategic, "big picture" thinker who understands the business model, the market, and the overall business plan. An operations person is someone who rolls up their sleeves, wades up to their hip boots in the details and executes the strategy that the visionary comes up with. You are either one or the other—it is almost impossible to be both. Once you have determined if you are a "visionary" or an "operations person," look for your opposite number. That way your business is more likely to strike the right balance between strategy and tactics.

Section 3

Do you have all the skills you need on board to make the business work? Perhaps you are an inventor who is excellent at product design but clueless about selling. Perhaps you have a strong marketing background but need someone to help you crunch the numbers and make sure your products or services can be delivered within budget. Your partners should complement your set of business skills, not duplicate them. Keep in mind that you can acquire someone's skills without making them a partner. If a particular skill, such as contract negotiation or bookkeeping, is not critical to the success of your business, you may be better off hiring a lawyer, accountant, or consultant to do it for you and keeping ownership of your business.

Section 4

Can you communicate directly and honestly with this person, without pulling any punches? Communication between partners can often get rough; disagreements and arguments break out all the time. It is difficult to criticize someone harshly, yet sometimes you must be cruel with your business partners in order to do the right thing for your business. Your business may well suffer if you consistently hold back important information for fear of offending your partner or jeopardizing the underlying friendship or emotional bond between you.

Section 5

Sometimes the most successful business partnerships are those where the partners do not socialize outside the office.

And lastly, is your business partner willing to hang around for the long haul? This is the critical test of a business partner. Many people are happy to help out with a business during its start-up phase, only to lose interest later on when something more attractive (like a job offer from a big corporation) comes along, a life-changing event (like the birth of a new child) occurs, or the going is getting tougher and the business isn't as much 'fun' as it used to be. If you are not sure if someone is committed to the long-term success of your business, make them an employee or independent contractor, with perhaps an 'option' to acquire an interest in your business at a date two or three years down the road . . . provided, of course, they are still working for you at that time and you continue to be satisfied with their performance.

1.25 (Page 64)

A: 98 percent of staff working at Blue Skies Recruitment say they laugh a lot with their team. As many as 95 percent say that they are excited about where the company is going. So what do they have to smile about? Last month this small San Francisco-based company won a prestigious award for being one of the best small companies to work for in the U.S. With us today is Will Counts, CEO of Blue Skies. Will, first of all, tell us a little bit more about the company and what you do.

B: Good morning. Well, Blue Skies is more than just a normal recruitment agency. The difference is that we actually train and then place college graduates in sales jobs. That means we have a lot of young people working for us, so it's a bit like a continuation of college, but with a salary. We're only a small company, with as few as sixty employees, but there's a great deal of energy in our office.

A: Yes, your employees have said that it's a fun atmosphere, with smart outgoing people. You have regular parties, an annual ski weekend, a present for the most-appreciated employee of the month, and plenty of other benefits. I'm not much of an expert on these things. Why such an emphasis on staff incentives?

B: Well, our employees are young and highly qualified. They are good at what they do, and they believe in it. We have trained sales people going into companies to try and place graduates. Quite a few of them get offered the job themselves. If we didn't treat our employees well, they would quickly get poached by other companies. So the incentives need to be good to keep people.

A: So how are your salaries?

B: Salaries are high and there are monthly, performance-related cash bonuses. Employees also set their own targets for the coming year, and for the most part they have a say in their incentives as well.

A: And how about the atmosphere in the office. How do you influence that?

B: We have a company café, where we offer free breakfasts, and cappuccino all day long. People spend a lot of time in there discussing ideas over coffee, but it's very productive.

A: The vast majority of your employees say that they admire their managers, and feel that they can actively contribute to the future success of the company. How did you achieve this?

B: Well, one of the things is that we help them with finding somewhere nice to live. Rent is very expensive in San Francisco, and as a lot of our employees are just fresh out of college, with a lot of debt, they don't have a large budget for rent. So, we bought some homes, and quite a few employees rent them from us at reasonable rates. It makes a real difference. It means that working for the company becomes a lifestyle choice. They are involved personally. Also, we like to give people a say in the company. We have monthly meetings to discuss big issues, when we all sit around and talk about things. Initially, only a handful of people would come to the meetings. So we decided to offer free food, sandwiches and pizza, and now everyone comes, and everyone has something to say.

1.26 (Page 64)

1. As many as 95 percent say that they are excited about where the company is going.
2. Will, first of all, tell us a little bit more about the company and what you do.
3. We're only a small company, with as few as sixty employees, but there's a great deal of energy in our office.
4. You have regular parties, an annual ski weekend, a present for the most-appreciated employee of the month, and plenty of other benefits.
5. I'm not much of an expert on these things.
6. Employees also set their own targets for the coming year, and for the most part they have a say in their incentives as well.
7. The vast majority of your employees say that they admire their managers.
8. So, we bought some homes, and quite a few employees rent them from us at reasonable rates.
9. Initially, only a handful of people would come to the meetings.

1.27 (Page 66)

A: Well, if we had a million dollars, I'd replace these chairs for a start. No wonder I've got a backache.

B: Oh come on, we can do better than that. How about an all-expense-paid trip to the Bahamas or something?

A: Would you really want to go on a vacation with our co-workers?

B: Well, no, but . . .

A: I think it should be spent on day-to-day things that'll make a difference here, like renovating the office.

B: That is so boring!

A: Or maybe . . . what d'you mean boring?!

B: Well, it's lots of money—let's have some fun! The company could get a house on the beach that the employees could use whenever they wanted.

A: Yes, but that would only be useful once every few years for each person. It wouldn't make the least bit of difference for most of us. My first priority would be to do something practical with the money . . .

ENGLISH in Common 6A

Workbook

Antonia Clare and JJ Wilson

Series Consultants
María Victoria Saumell and Sarah Louisa Birchley

ALWAYS LEARNING PEARSON

UNIT 1
Achieving goals

LESSON 1

Reading

1a Read the article. What makes Mark Inglis unusual?

____

____

Testing the Limits

On May 15, 2006, a boyhood dream came true for Mark Inglis, a mountain climber from New Zealand. He had always wanted to stand on the roof of the world. At the age of 47, he became the first man with two artificial legs to reach the summit of Mount Everest, the highest mountain in the world at 29,092 feet (8,848 meters).

In 1982, as a search and rescue mountain guide, Mark was trapped in a blizzard for two weeks on Mount Cook, the highest mountain in New Zealand. Both legs were amputated due to frostbite. After recovering, Mark went on to become a medical scientist in leukemia research, a winemaker, and an inspiring motivational speaker.

Being a double amputee has never slowed him down. He has been able to ski and has always loved cycling. He won a silver medal in cycling in the 2000 Sydney Paralympic games. He then returned to that same mountain where he lost his legs to finish the climb he started twenty years ago.

After conquering Mount Cook, he went on to climb Mount Cho Oyu in Tibet, the world's sixth highest peak at 26, 901 feet (8,201 meters). From the summit of Cho Oyu, he looked out at Everest and decided that would be his next challenge. He was able to make the climb on two carbon-fiber artificial legs, designed especially for climbing. One of his artificial limbs snapped on the way up the mountain, but he was able to repair it quickly with the tools and the spare leg parts he had brought with him.

Though his voice was shaky and it was difficult to speak on the top of Mount Everest, he was able to call his wife Anne and share his great news. She said, "He's dreamed of this all his life . . . "

Helen Clark, the New Zealand Prime Minister, also an amateur climber, officially congratulated Mark for his great accomplishment. She said that he had sent a message to other people with disabilities "that your ambitions should never be limited."

Because of the Everest climb he was able to raise tens of thousands of dollars for the Cambodia Trust, an organization that helps amputees. Recently he created a new charity called Limbs4All, which is working to help 400 million disabled people in the world.

b Mark the sentences true (*T*) or false (*F*).

____ 1. Mark Inglis had both legs amputated due to frostbite in 1982.

____ 2. He never found the courage to return to climb the mountain where he lost his legs.

____ 3. On reaching the top of Everest, Mark was completely unable to speak.

____ 4. The Prime Minister of New Zealand congratulated Mark on his achievement.

____ 5. Mark broke one of his artificial legs while climbing down the mountain.

____ 6. Mark successfully climbed Mount Cook and Mount Cho Oyu before attempting Mount Everest.

____ 7. Before his legs were amputated Mark had also won a silver medal for cycling.

2a Complete the questions with words from the box.

make	set	ambition	rising
without	face	attitude	

1. What achievable goals did Mark ____________?
2. What challenges did he ____________?
3. Did Mark succeed in ____________ to the challenge?
4. How did he ____________ his dream come true?
5. What couldn't Mark have done it ____________?
6. What advice did the Prime Minister give to people with an ultimate ____________?
7. Do you think Mark had the right ____________?

b Answer the questions in Exercise 2a on a separate sheet of paper.

Grammar

3 Circle the correct choice.

1. We finally opted _to/for/on_ the silver color.
2. It is a method of distinguishing cancer cells _from/between/of_ normal tissue.
3. Very few people succeed _on losing/to lose/in losing_ weight and keeping it off.
4. His headaches stemmed _from/with/to_ vision problems.
5. It is most likely to appeal _at/to/with_ the younger generation.
6. We all came to rely _on/in/with_ her judgment.
7. We want him to get the maximum benefit _of/from/with_ the class.
8. The wall of the prison was riddled _of/in/with_ bullet holes.
9. She seems to be lacking _with/on/in_ confidence.

Vocabulary

4 Complete the conversations with words from the box.

delight	cram	master
picked	linguistic ability	

1. **A:** I didn't know you could speak Thai!
   B: I can't really. I just ____________ up a few words while I was there on vacation.
2. **A:** How long did it take you to ____________ the grammar?
   B: Years! I had to ____________ a lot of information into my brain.
3. **A:** What do you enjoy most about being able to speak Russian?
   B: The sheer ____________ of being able to talk to people I meet there.
4. **A:** I can't believe how quickly she's learned the language.
   B: Yes, she has an amazing ____________.

Reading

5 Read the article. Then answer the questions on a separate sheet of paper.

Languages and the brain

Research has shown that people with a gift for languages could actually have different types of brains from other people.

In a recent trial involving native French speakers, people were asked to distinguish between two similar sounds from different languages. The first was the /d/ sound found in French. The second was a /d/ found in Hindi, which is pronounced in a different way. Researchers tested the speed at which participants could process the information about the different sounds. People who were successful in this task were asked to listen to other similar sounds.

Some of the fastest learners were able to tell the sounds apart within a few minutes, while the slowest learners were only able to make random guesses after 20 minutes of training.

Dr. Narly Golestani, from the University College London's Institute of Cognitive Neuroscience, said the brain's white matter was involved in the efficient processing of sound information. Its fibers are involved in connecting brain regions together. Fast language learners had a greater volume of white matter, and that may mean they have more, or perhaps thicker, fibers.

"We are starting to understand that brain shape and structure can be informative about people's abilities—why people are good at some things and not others is evident from these scans," she said.

"This latest research could be used in other ways," Dr. Golestani said. "We can start to make predictions regarding whether people will be good at something or not based on their brain structure or even to diagnose clinical problems."

1. What do scientists hope to achieve through the new research?
2. What did people have to distinguish between during the trial?
3. How did the researchers decide who was a "good" language learner?
4. What is the function of fibers in the brain's white matter?
5. What can you tell from the brain scans?

LESSON 2

Vocabulary

1 Match the beginning of the sentence with its end.

____ **1.**	We had to learn poems by	**a.**	head, I'd say there were about 50.
____ **2.**	I grew up here. I know it like the back	**b.**	of my hand.
____ **3.**	I know next to	**c.**	David Marshall?
____ **4.**	Just off the top of my	**d.**	heart when I was in school.
____ **5.**	I'm pretty	**e.**	what time the show starts?
____ **6.**	Have you ever heard of	**f.**	sure he'll say yes.
____ **7.**	Lee knew the game	**g.**	nothing about antiques.
____ **8.**	Do you know offhand	**h.**	inside out.

Grammar

2 Read the article. Underline examples of passives and other verbs used for distancing.

Notable lasts

1. Lillian Asplund, who died at age 99, was the last American survivor of the Titanic, and the only living person with any memory of the events of April 15, 1912. She was five years old when the ship went down in the freezing waters of the north Atlantic, taking with it her father and three of her brothers. As she was pulled to safety in a lifeboat, she saw them peering at her over the ship's railing. The image is said to have haunted her for the rest of her life, and despite the world's ongoing fascination with the Titanic, it seems she rarely spoke of the tragedy.

2. Martha is thought to have been the last surviving passenger pigeon. Passenger pigeons were probably once the most common bird in the world. It is estimated that there were as many as five billion passenger pigeons in the United States. They lived in enormous flocks, sometimes up to a mile wide and 300 miles long, taking several days to pass and probably containing two billion birds. They were hunted to extinction by humans. Martha, the last of her species, died in the Cincinnati Zoo in 1914. She was then frozen in a block of ice and her body was sent to The Smithsonian Institution, where she can still be seen.

3. Ishi was the name given to the last member of the Yahi tribe of California, and means "man" in the Yahi language. Ishi is believed to be the last Native American in Northern California to have lived the bulk of his life completely outside the European American culture. He was thought to have left his homeland in the foothills near Lassen Peak, California, and was found when he emerged from the wild on August 29, 1911. His real name was never known, because in his society it was taboo to say one's own name. Since he was the last member of his tribe, his real name died with him.

3 Complete the paragraphs using passives and the verbs in parentheses. Add extra words if necessary.

It ______________ (1. say) that Thomas Edison, the famous inventor, believed that taking off one's clothing caused insomnia. It ______________ (2. seem) that he often slept in his clothes on newspapers beneath the stairs in his laboratory.

Alexander Graham Bell, inventor of the telephone, ______________ (3. claim) to have first answered the device by saying "hoy, hoy" instead of "hello"!

Charles Goodyear, who ______________ (4. say) to have been instrumental in establishing the rubber industry in the US, ______________ (5. think) to have carried out his first experiments in jail.

Leonardo da Vinci ______________ (6. think) to have designed a military tank in the fifteenth century. Remarkably, he ______________ (7. believe) to have also worked on designs for hot-air balloons and deep-sea diving suits.

Joseph Merlin, a Belgian musician, invented roller skates in 1760. He ______________ (8. appear) to have first demonstrated them at a ball by skating across the room playing a violin.

Reading

4a Read the news clippings. Circle the key words.

For the second year in a row, the city of Luanda, Angola, has beaten Tokyo for the title of "world's most expensive city." The city is pricey because there is little competition and few items are produced locally. Interestingly, although Luanda is very expensive, over half of the Angolan population lives in poverty.

Crime in many US cities, including Washington D.C., has decreased in recent years. Local authorities credit better policing and technology for the drop. Thanks to mobile technology, law enforcement can receive up-to-date reports on criminal activity and emergencies in their patrol areas. In D.C., this has resulted in the lowest crime rates in forty years.

Tourism officials are reminding visitors to China to be vigilant and to keep an eye on their surroundings and belongings. This warning comes after video surveillance caught several Chinese pickpockets stealing wallets and cell phones using chopsticks. These bold thieves target inattentive passersby and dip into their pockets with the wooden utensils.

Teens in some parts of Philadelphia are now subject to a 9:00 P.M. curfew. The curfew was established because groups of teens have been harassing other citizens and disturbing local businesses. These groups have been organizing their criminal acts using text messaging and social media websites like Twitter and Facebook.

b Answer the questions on a separate sheet of paper.

1. How can the lack of locally-made products drive up prices in a city?
2. How do you think police can use technology to prevent crime?
3. What are some ways to keep your belongings safe from pickpockets?
4. What are some good and bad uses for social media?

LESSON 3

Reading

1a Read the interview on the right. Then answer the questions.

1. What kinds of races does Annie compete in?
2. What is her ambition?
3. How did her parents influence her?
4. What injuries has she suffered?
5. How does she cope when she is hurt?

b Find words or expressions in the reading that mean:

1. only just (paragraph 1) ______________
2. something she really wants to achieve (paragraph 2) ______________
3. be an equally strong competitor (paragraph 2) ______________
4. be very eager to do something (paragraph 4) ______________
5. be able to do (paragraph 5) ______________
6. give up (paragraph 6) ______________

c Complete the sentences. Use the correct form of the words and phrases from Exercise 1b.

1. He is extremely ambitious. His ______________ is to take over the whole company.
2. My job is getting so stressful, I'm thinking about ______________.
3. They had ______________ exited the office when the police arrived.
4. The Mexican team is very talented and will prove to be a ______________ for the Canadians.
5. I was ______________ for an adventure, so I signed up for a trip across Africa.
6. I'm not sure that they're entirely ______________ finishing the job.

Nerves of steel

1 She's blond, charming, enthusiastic, and above all, extremely determined. If you judge Annie Seel only by her looks, you're in for the greatest of surprises. There are other women motorcyclists for sure, but how many crave extreme adventure in such a way, and how many single-handedly take on all the toughest rallies the world has to offer? Addicted early on to speed and adrenaline, the desert princess switched from horses to motorcycle races when she was barely 16.

2 After 20 years and 17 broken bones, she continues to try to quench her thirst for success and for new records to break, as much at home up Mount Everest as on African rallies, on tarmac races as on Mexican bajas. Can you guess the ultimate quest for this woman? To be a true match for her male counterparts in the greatest races, starting with a race called the Rallye du Maroc, in which she's riding in the marathon class.

3 **Annie, what gave you this taste for extreme adventure?**

"I grew up next to a racecourse. I quickly got addicted to speed, and then at 16, I saw some motorcycle stuntmen at a show. I was awed. I bought myself a motorcycle, but none of my friends liked speed as much as I did. Then, when I was 18, I started to do road racing and finished eighth in the Swedish Championships . . ."

4 **And in 2000 you tried a rally in Dubai . . .**

"I went to Morocco and fell in love with the desert. I was desperate to do a race. I ordered a DIY Husaberg 600 and assembled it barely ten days before the start.

5 I rode on my own and made straight for the sand dunes. On the last day, I got a fractured foot but I still got to the finish in 49th place. Since then, I've been to Tunisia and Argentina. This Moroccan race is my sixth one in the World Championships. I'm trying to show what I'm capable of doing with the hope of finding some money for the Dakar race. To tell you the truth, it's fairly hard to find any money in Sweden for these kinds of races . . ."

6 **What's most impressive about you is your determination. You've broken your bones 17 times, yet you've never given up.**

"No, I never quit. My father, who died when I was 16, gave me a taste for mechanical things, and my mother gave me exceptionally strong will power. When I broke my hand on the fourth stage of the Dakar in 2002, I held on until the end. My left leg had gone blue all over. I'll admit, though, that I've always been lucky enough to have injuries that didn't prevent me from finishing the race. When I run into a problem, I scream a little and then I go on."

Vocabulary

2 Complete the sentences with words from the box.

pushing	faces	pursue	heading	deal

1. You need to keep your priorities straight if you want to __________ your dream.
2. The president __________ the difficult task of putting the economy back on its feet.
3. My tutor was always __________ me to do better.
4. We have had to __________ with a lot of unnecessary criticism.
5. I'm worried they may be __________ for trouble.

Grammar

3 Complete the article using the correct form of the verbs in parentheses.

Dutch motorcycle rider Martin Jansen is a very calm and patient man. By the end of this year he __________ (**1.** be) on the road for over 30 years. This hardworking and determined biker, who __________ (**2.** travel) a quarter of a million miles, through 100 different countries, arrived in Vancouver last week. Shortly after arriving on the ferry from the Granville Islands, the motorcycle that __________ (**3.** be) his constant companion for 30 years was stolen. However, Martin took it in stride. After all, he couldn't __________ (**4.** spend) all those years riding around the world without learning a little patience.

Actually, his motorcycle __________ (**5.** be returned) to him just 24 hours after its theft. Jansen somehow knew he would get it back. Before this, the bike __________ already __________ (**6.** be stolen) on three previous occasions. The last time __________ (**7.** be) in 2000. He thinks that having your motorcycle stolen almost every ten years is not too bad, considering how long he __________ (**8.** be) traveling.

This is not the only problem Jansen __________ (**9.** have) to deal with. Since he __________ (**10.** give up) his job as an auto mechanic in Pennsylvania and set off on his journey, Jansen __________ (**11.** be hit) three times by cars, and __________ even __________ (**12.** break) both legs. He earns money by writing and selling books about his travels. But he __________ often __________ (**13.** be) hungry. His life has been an incredible experience, and he is looking forward to many more adventures.

Writing

4 Write a paragraph about a personal achievement or about another person's achievement that you particularly admire. Use a separate sheet of paper.

Ideas:
career, health
family, travel
sports, school
fulfilling a dream

UNIT 1 Review

1 Circle the correct word or phrase to complete each sentence.

1. It is widely ___ eating too many fatty foods causes heart disease.
   - a. believing
   - b. to be believed of
   - c. believed that
   - d. believed to be
2. The notes from last month's meeting ___ lost.
   - a. are appeared
   - b. seem to have be
   - c. appear that they are
   - d. seem to have been
3. It seems ___ Mr. Klein was wrong about the figures.
   - a. that
   - b. if
   - c. as to
   - d. as
4. Is the shipment ___ this afternoon?
   - a. be delivered
   - b. being delivered
   - c. deliver
   - d. to deliver
5. Smoking ___ allowed on planes for years.
   - a. isn't being
   - b. isn't
   - c. hasn't been
   - d. doesn't
6. ___ in the past that the world was flat?
   - a. Was there assumed
   - b. Did it assume
   - c. Was assumed
   - d. Was it assumed
7. Carlos ___ the most handsome man in Buenos Aires society.
   - a. has said to be
   - b. was said to be
   - c. was to be
   - d. was said
8. The company ___ gone bankrupt because of increased competition.
   - a. is thought
   - b. is said to be
   - c. said to have
   - d. is thought to have

2 Match the beginning of the sentence with its end.

___ 1. She is said to	a. made by now.
___ 2. It was widely	b. if you've just seen a ghost.
___ 3. The robbers were thought	c. to have escaped.
___ 4. Judging by this map, we appear to have	d. be a genius.
___ 5. It seems as though	e. be submitted by tomorrow.
___ 6. You look as	f. the weather will get better.
___ 7. The competition entry must	g. become completely lost.
___ 8. The wedding cake will have been	h. assumed that Minsoo would inherit his father's money.

3 Complete each sentence using the correct perfect form of the verb in parentheses.

1. By this time next week we ____________ school, and I'll be on vacation! (finish)
2. It was only when Mariana told me her name that I realized we ________ before. (meet)
3. The children were all sunburned. They ____________ football in the sun all day. (play)
4. She looks exhausted because she ________ well recently. (not sleep)
5. By next July, Kazunari probably ____________ his thesis. (write)
6. Yesterday, Mr. Jones finally received his visa. He ____________ to get one for years. (try)
7. Wow! Fantastic news! I ________ a scholarship to the university. (win)
8. We went to a Mowgli concert. I ________ of them before, but they were very good. (not hear)
9. By tomorrow, Don ____________ here for over fifty years! He started as an assistant. (be)

4 Is the sentence in *italics* replying to statement **a** or **b**?

1. a. We haven't been feeding the cat enough food.
   b. We haven't fed the cat enough food.
   ___ *I know. He's started catching mice again recently.*
2. a. How many countries will you have visited after this trip?
   b. How many countries will you visit on this trip?
   ___ *If you include the one where I was born, then 18!*
3. a. We haven't been told the schedule.
   b. We hadn't been told the schedule.
   ___ *Well, I think the conference starts at 9:00, and you're speaking at 11:00.*
4. a. I've been sitting quietly, minding my own business.
   b. I'd been sitting quietly, minding my own business.
   ___ *And then what happened?*
5. a. Where have you put the money?
   b. Where will you have put the money?
   ___ *I put it where you told me to.*

5 Complete the article with the correct form of words from the box plus a preposition.

opt	appeal	succeed	benefit
rely	bother	nervous	
short	subject	reminiscent	

Vacation Challenge is guaranteed to ______________ (**1.**) your adventurous spirit. We provide a choice of parachute jumps, hang gliding, rock climbing and kayaking. You can ______________ (**2.**) two sports plus luxury accommodations and food for just $300 a week! Or, if you're ______________ (**3.**) cash, you can choose the economy camping option for $175.

What if you are ______________ (**4.**) trying a new sport? Don't worry. You can ______________ (**5.**) us to provide the best training available to ensure that you're safe. And we won't ________ you ________ (**6.**) any 5:00 A.M. mornings or boot camp horrors! Read what our customers have said about us.

"I really ______________ (**7.**) my two weeks with Vacation Challenge. It was an amazing experience!" (*Cal Jones, New York*)

"It was ______________ (**8.**) my childhood: running around, learning new stuff, without a care in the world. The best vacation I've ever had." (*Young-Chul, Korea*)

"Don't ______________ (**9.**) checking the competitors. Vacation Challenge is the one." (*Sanath Kuppara, Sri Lanka*)

"I ______________ (**10.**) living my dreams! Thank you, Vacation Challenge." (*Macarena Duval, Chile*)

6 Add or cross out one word to complete each sentence.

1. Paulo Freire? Who's he? I've never heard him.
2. The Whorf-Sapir hypothesis? I know it like in the back of my hand.
3. Wendy's phone number? I don't know it by offhand.
4. Shakespeare's love poems? We spent years learning them by the heart.
5. Rules in the driving manual? Ask Susie—she's a driving instructor. She knows it inside.
6. International banking? I know next nothing about it.

7 Number the lines 1–11 to put them in the correct order.

__*1*__ Climber Rheinhold Messner always knew that he had the
____ challenge. Most doctors and scientists suggested that this was not an achievable
____ come true with a successful three-day ascent.
____ all expectations. After a few months' preparation, Messner pursued his dream
____ something truly amazing in the mountains. However, in 1980, he exceeded
____ of risk about climbing Everest, but Messner's attempt to take
____ of being the first man to ascend Everest without oxygen supplies. There is always an element
____ potential to accomplish
____ on the world's highest mountain without
____ goal. Against all expectations, on August 20, he made his dream
____ oxygen was a real

UNIT 2

Places and communities

LESSON 1

Communication

1a Read about three students' embarrassing moments abroad. Complete the chart.

	Speaker 1	Speaker 2	Speaker 3
1. Nationality of speaker			
2. Country where embarrassing moment happened			
3. Main problem			
4. Speaker's final thoughts about the situation			

Embarrassing moments

Speaker 1

After a long journey from Vancouver, I was really happy to have arrived at my host family's house in Colombia. They were extremely friendly, even though I spoke only a little Spanish, and they plied me with lemonade and made me feel comfortable. After a while, the mother asked me, "Estas casado"? I thought she was asking me if I was tired, so I said: "Si, un poco," which means "yes, a little." Suddenly everyone laughed. Later I found out that "casado" means married, and "cansado" means tired. So she'd asked me if I was married and I'd said: "Oh, a little"! That was just the first of many linguistic blunders I made! Actually, looking back, I wish I'd learned more of the language before moving there, but I did pick it up pretty quickly.

Speaker 2

I'm from Argentina, but I've lived in the US for ten years. When I first got a car, I needed to buy gas, so I drove to a gas station and sat there waiting to be served. And I sat there, and I sat there, and no one came. Eventually, a little perplexed, I went into the store and asked for a full tank of gas. The girl took my money, and I went back to the car and waited again. Still, no one came. So I thought maybe someone had done it for me while I was in the store. So I drove off. But then I looked at the gas gauge and the tank was completely empty. I drove back to the gas station and suddenly I realized I had to fill the car myself. I've never done this before, because in Argentina the people who work at the gas station do it for you. I felt a little bit stupid, as you can imagine.

Speaker 3

This was before I could speak English well. I was flying back to Italy, and I was at JFK Airport. For some reason, I didn't have my glasses. I'm very short sighted so I couldn't see the information on the screen. So I asked someone official-looking, "Which gate for Milan?" and he said: "It's too early. There's no gate." I got confused because I thought that "early" meant "late," so I began to panic, thinking I'd missed my flight. So I asked someone else, and again: "You're too early. No gate assigned. You'll have to wait." And I was tearing my hair out and wondering why these Americans were so calm when I'd just missed my flight. Eventually, a nice American man explained, very pleasantly, that the gate number would appear very soon and that I hadn't missed my flight. He was probably thinking: "Dumb tourist." So the moral of the story is: learn the basics. And don't lose your glasses!

b Find words or phrases in the reading that mean:

1. give someone large amounts of food or drink (Speaker 1) ________
2. careless mistakes (Speaker 1) ________
3. confused by something (Speaker 2) ________
4. formal word for *given*, for example, a task or a seat (Speaker 3) ________
5. idiom for going crazy or getting angry (Speaker 3) ________

Grammar

2 Circle the correct choice.

1. The travel agency recommends _to take/taking/take_ traveler's checks rather than cash.
2. We look forward to _meet/meeting/have met_ you in June.
3. My parents always encouraged me _that write/writing/to write_ down my thoughts.
4. After graduating, Melissa thought _of travel/of traveling/to travel_ for a year, but decided against it.
5. Mark recommended _ride/her to ride/riding_ a bicycle as a good way to get in shape.
6. They couldn't afford _to waste/that they waste/wasting_ time on trivial matters.
7. I would urge _to reconsider/you to reconsider/you reconsider_ the offer before it's too late.
8. We've avoided _to do/that we do/doing_ anything too dangerous so far.
9. I object _I have to/to having to/I have to_ pay for my own travel to these conferences.
10. Chiara persuaded _us that we go/us go/us to go_ on a boat trip with her.

3 Match the beginning of the sentence with its end.

____ 1. The Taj Mahal really is a must-
____ 2. Disney World is a superb value
____ 3. The hotel is nice, but it's
____ 4. Everyone says the museum is amazing, but in my view it's not
____ 5. If I were you, I'd
____ 6. You should try
____ 7. Make sure
____ 8. Watch out

a. for mosquitoes, and take your malaria pills.
b. backpacking because it's cheap.
c. see because it's so beautiful.
d. all it's cracked up to be.
e. go in April, when it isn't too hot.
f. a little overpriced.
g. you go to Macchu Pichu.
h. for the money.

4 Complete the article using the correct form of verbs from the box. Add extra words where necessary.

try	hear	make	object	find out
live	think	advise	afford	change

Culture shock

Those people thinking ______________ (1.) abroad will face a number of challenges, including communication difficulties and settling in to a new community. But perhaps the biggest challenge is culture shock. You may find yourself ______________ (2.) to everything about the host culture: the way the people drive, wait in line, greet you, their habits, and attitudes toward everything around you, such as litter and personal space. This is common. People cannot avoid ______________ (3.) that their own culture does things "the right way." Everything else is therefore wrong. We urge you ______________ (4.) your mindset. There are no cultural rights or wrongs, only differences. What's more, if you're committed to staying in a foreign country for more than a few days, you can't ______________ (5.) be critical of everything around you. It'll make your life miserable.

The greatest divider of nations is ignorance, and so the first solution is knowledge. We recommend ______________ (6.) as much as you can about the host culture before you arrive—its customs, people, priorities, and manners. When you've done your homework, if you really can't imagine ______________ (7.) a new life there, go somewhere else.

We also encourage you ______________ (8.) to see that diversity is interesting. No one would really want to live in a world in which every culture was the same, so we ______________ (9.) you to observe and enjoy the differences. Eventually you will come to accept them.

We look forward ______________ (10.) from you about your experiences.

5 Make the sentences more polite using the words in parentheses.

1. Can you turn down the music? (mind)
   Would ______________ down the music?
2. Can you hand in your essay first thing tomorrow? (think)
   ______________ you could hand in your essay first thing tomorrow?
3. Can I come? (possible)
   Would ______________ for me to come?
4. Ideally, you could help us move our things out of the house. (hoping)
   We ______________ you could help us move our things out of the house.

Grammar

1a Read Articles 1 and 2 and complete the sentence.

Article 1 is _______ positive about Wikipedia _______ Article 2.

for your information . . .

We question the facts so you know the truth

1

Wikipedia has revolutionized the way encyclopedias are compiled. Its open nature has led to a democratizing process; knowledge is now not only in the hands of professors, but of the ordinary man or woman who has the interest, time, and dedication to research and document facts. No wonder the establishment feels threatened. "It's not authoritative!" they cry. "It's too left-wing!" "It doesn't represent the whole range of culture!" Of course it doesn't. It is a contemporary comment on the world. With time, today's contributors' views will be challenged and edited by a new generation.

2

Wikipedia is a valuable resource for the amateur researcher in a hurry. If you want to find out when the Crimean War started, or what *quarks* are or when Picasso painted *Guernica*, Wikipedia will tell you, with 99.99% accuracy. But for anything more complex, Wikipedia is full of potential or real misinformation. It's not the contributors' fault; they genuinely want to get it right. But, for all we know, the contributors could be five-year-olds. Wikipedia's open-source system means that anyone—young children, obsessives, and the lunatic fringe—can edit it. Because of this, no serious academic should trust Wikipedia.

next week we discuss . . .

b Correct the mistake in each sentence.

1. It is not near as complimentary about Wikipedia as the other article.
2. It suggests that Wikipedia is not nearly like as reliable as other encyclopedias.
3. It is more considerably positive about Wikipedia than the other article.
4. According to Article 2, the less we know about the contributors, less we can trust Wikipedia.
5. The author of one article is definitely not as critical of Wikipedia to the author of the other article.
6. One article implies that it's far to let everyone contribute to encyclopedias.

2a Replace the words and expressions in *italics* with words and expressions from the box. You will not use all of them.

concerning	would like
Yours sincerely	following
of your attendance	take place
a previous arrangement	be grateful
look forward to hearing	Dear
don't hesitate to contact me	

___ 1. We *hope to hear* from you soon. _______________

___ 2. Please *get in touch* if you have any questions. _______________

___ 3. *Hi*, Mrs. Dormer, _______________

___ 4. Technics Solutions *wants* to invite you to our annual investors' meeting _______________

___ 5. inform us *whether you will be able to come* by June 14. _______________

___ 6. which will *be* at The Atrium on Rose Street at 5:00 on July 6. _______________

___ 7. We would *like it* if you could _______________

___ 8. *Best wishes*, _______________

b Number the sentences in the correct order to make a formal letter.

Reading

3a Read the articles. Which community did each website target?

___ **a.** Fashionable people ___ **c.** Readers

___ **b.** People who have things to sell

1

Pierre Omidyar, the son of French-Iranian immigrants, was already a millionaire before launching eBay. Omidyar's electronics site, e-shop, was bought out by Microsoft in 1996, making him a millionaire before he'd turned 30. With this money, he set up an online auction company that allowed people to show items they wished to sell; other users then made a bid. Omidyar wanted to name the site Echo Bay Technology Group. This name was already owned by a Canadian mining company, so he shortened the name to eBay®, and a legend was born. Almost immediately, eBay made a profit. The site sold goods ranging from computers to posters to underwear. The growth of eBay was phenomenal. It is now the world's most successful online business, and its users consider themselves part of a distinct community. Over 150 million registered users buy and sell goods worth $1,050 every second. The website is used by big companies such as Vodaphone and IBM to sell off excess stock, but the majority of goods still sell for less than $50.

2

It was the early 90s, the Internet boom was just beginning, and Jeff Bezos wanted to be a part of this brave, new, forward-thinking community. After leaving his job on Wall Street, Bezos decided to set up an online bookselling business. Using his garage in Seattle as an office, Bezos created Amazon.com. The idea was to make the buying of books cheap and easy, with more choices than the traditional bookstore could provide. The site had a number of features that made it attractive to potential users: fast service, search capabilities, low costs for users, tools for comparing prices of books, and personalization in the form of customer-written book reviews. As a 24-hour virtual bookstore, Amazon was convenient, cheap, and reliable. Gradually, through word-of-mouth, the company grew in popularity. Bezos had originally handled customer orders himself, but he soon realized that the company was growing too fast for one man. By 1998, the net sales were $540 million, and a whole generation of book buyers was hooked.

3

Ernst Malmsten, an events organizer, and Kajsa Leander, a supermodel, grew up in Lund, Sweden. In the late 90s, they decided to launch boo.com, a website that would create a global fashion community by selling designer clothes all over the world.

From the beginning, there were difficulties. Clothing companies didn't trust the Internet and were reluctant to sell online. Also, no one was sure that people would buy clothes without trying them on first. On November 3,1999, the day boo.com was launched, the website had 25,000 hits, but these resulted in only eight actual orders for clothes. Worse, a well-known journalist wrote a negative article about boo.com, explaining how it had taken him 81 minutes to order a product. Other problems included viruses and a fraud detection system that rejected customers' orders. By March 2000, half of boo.com's workforce had lost their jobs. While most Internet start-ups are run from garages or bedrooms, boo.com had luxurious offices in six of the world's most glamorous and expensive cities. Fresh fruit and flowers were delivered daily. Malmsten and Leander, who always traveled first-class, claimed that companies in the fashion industry needed this image. But boo.com was spending faster than it was earning, and the company was doomed.

b Are these statements true about Amazon, eBay, or boo.com?

1. The founder originally wanted a different name for the website. ___
2. The company had a high-class, stylish image. ___
3. Users of the site could post their own opinions of the things being sold. ___
4. The site sold a range of goods from the beginning. ___
5. The type of item for sale wasn't ideal for online shopping. ___
6. The founder or founders originally ran the website alone. ___
7. The founder or founders was or were already rich before launching the website. ___
8. The company had some technical problems. ___

c Find words in the articles that mean:

1. offer of a price for something (*v., n.*) (Article 1) ___
2. extraordinary or remarkable (*adj.*) (Article 1) ___
3. a store of goods ready for sale (*n.*) (Article 1) ___
4. unwilling or not wanting to do something (*adj.*) (Article 3) ___
5. new company (especially Internet companies) (*n.*) (Article 3) ___
6. extremely comfortable and expensive (*adj.*) (Article 3) ___
7. destined to end badly (*adj.*) (Article 3) ___

Reading

1a Read about three different communities. What positive aspects of each community are described?

Positive aspects:

Community 1 ______________________________

Community 2 ______________________________

Community 3 ______________________________

Community 1

People might think that because our community is poor, the people are unhappy, or maybe there's nothing to do. But that's really not the case at all. All kinds of things go on within the townships; each one is really a real hive of activity. For example, one of the ways we entertain ourselves is through music. Music brings people together, and of course it's free. There are so many choirs here I've lost count, and they don't just sing our traditional songs; they do all sorts of other things like pop and classical music. A visitor once left us a tape of Robbie Williams, and we learned the songs and sing the harmonies. Another activity that's important here is soccer. Again, the beauty of it is that it's free and anyone can play. The girls have a team, and there's an over-60s team. The field where we play used to be covered with broken glass and had animals grazing, but we fixed it, and now it's very good. And whenever Bafana Bafana plays, we all sit around one television and cheer and sing. So, life in a township is hard, of course, but we have a way of making the best out of the things we have. No one sits around feeling sorry for himself.

Community 2

My grandfather once told me a saying. He said that the land doesn't belong to the people; the people belong to the land. I think this idea is one of the reasons why Vanuatu is special. The people are close to nature, and the nature here really is wonderful. Vanuatu is made up of lots of small islands, and we have beautiful coastlines and rainforests. The land is so fertile that we grow most of our own food, and this means that even the many poor people here won't starve. We are a close-knit community. People tend to help each other perhaps more than in built-up, developed communities. I remember a few years ago an American was stranded on one of the islands with his ten-year-old son because of a problem with the airline. I think he was a researcher. There were no stores or hotels, but the people here fed them and looked after them for three weeks until they could fly out. This is quite normal in Vanuatu. We are a spiritual people, and not very materialistic. We enjoy what we have and don't really seek material things. I hope that is how the world sees us, although I'm told that we are more famous for inventing bungee jumping!

Community 3

We were fed up with the "annoyances" of living in a regular community, so we decided to set up our own. Four years ago a group of 28 of us, all retired and all over 65, bought up some real estate and had the whole community designed and laid out for us. And this is the result. We have nothing at all against young people. In fact, most of us have children and grandchildren. But we just wanted a quiet neighborhood without noise and trash, and it works incredibly well. We are all old friends, and we have complementary skills. Jack down the road knows how to fix a car, and I used to work in real-estate law, so I deal with those issues. Reuben Barrios next door was a gardener, so he tells everyone how to grow flowers. It's everything we wanted for our old age. Our grandchildren visit us on the weekends, and we have a lot of fun, but come Monday, they're gone, and it's back to a quiet life.

b Mark the statements true (*T*) or false (*F*).

Community 1

_____ 1. The writer is from a rich area.

_____ 2. The hobbies there don't cost anything.

_____ 3. The people of the community are probably close and do many things together.

Community 2

_____ 4. Vanuatu is a place of natural beauty.

_____ 5. Most of the people of Vanuatu are wealthy.

_____ 6. The writer thinks that the people of Vanuatu are becoming more materialistic.

Community 3

_____ 7. The writer probably likes loud music.

_____ 8. The community is made up of friends.

_____ 9. The writer wishes there were more young people in the community.

c Choose the best definition.

Community 1

1. a real hive of activity
   a. full of action and productivity
   b. a place where people meet
   c. an appropriate time to do something
2. Bafana Bafana
   a. an African game
   b. a soccer team
   c. a type of music

Community 2

3. fertile
   a. beautiful and full of color
   b. free for everyone to use
   c. good for growing plants and food
4. stranded
   a. very hungry
   b. in trouble with the police
   c. couldn't get out

Community 3

5. real estate
   a. a very large house
   b. a plan made by an architect
   c. property such as houses or land
6. complementary
   a. saying how good something is
   b. the best
   c. (things) go well together, though they are different

Vocabulary

2 Complete the article with words from the box.

unspoiled	diverse	tranquil	views
magnificent	run-down	packed	vast
off the beaten track			

www.travelblogs.com/jilland

Traveling Sisters: The Travel Blog of Rachel and Gina

Days 12 and 13: Chiang Mai, Thailand

Greetings from Chiang Mai! Gina and I arrived early Saturday evening, which was perfect timing. Our hotel was very clean and modern, unlike the _____________ (1.) place we stayed at in Bangkok! The clerk recommended that we visit the nearby Saturday Walking Street. This market is _____________ (2.) and far from other sites. It wasn't very _____________ (3.), probably because few tourists know about it. The vendors had a _____________ (4.) array of items. There were locally produced silks, in a rainbow of _____________ (5.) colors. The quality was amazing, and after a little bargaining, so were the prices. I bought a gorgeous blue and green scarf. We also saw some incredible woodcarvings, a specialty in Chiang Mai.

It just so happened that we had arrived during the Loi Krathong festival, an event that happens each November. After strolling through the market, we bought two *krathongs*, small cups made with banana leaves and lotus flowers. People put coins or hair in them. At night, they light candles on the krathongs and float them down waterways. The cups carry away bad luck. People also light paper lanterns, which float into the _____________ (6.) night sky. Gina and I stood with the locals and watched. As I gazed at the lights, I just knew it was one of the most stunning _____________ (7.) I had ever seen!

The next morning, Gina and I explored the Old City, an area of town _____________ (8.) by modern architecture. Surrounded by ancient walls and a moat, the Old City is home to many *wats*, or temples. We stepped out of the noisy city streets and into the quiet of these _____________ (9.) spaces. We even met some monks! They were very friendly and eager to practice their English. It was a great way to spend our first full day in Chiang Mai.

UNIT 2
Review

1 Circle the correct choice.

1. The problem with Monaco is that the *price/cost/rate* of living is so high.
2. Buenos Aires has a *mild/calm/normal* climate. It isn't boiling in summer or freezing in winter.
3. The *health/medical/healthcare* system in Cuba used to be excellent, with many top hospitals.
4. Arguably, the highest *standard/rate/style* of living is found in Scandinavian countries.
5. For several years the crime *level/statistics/rate* in New York has been falling.
6. Apart from the air *uncleanness/pollution/dirt*, Mexico City is wonderful.
7. The best thing about Tokyo is its fantastic cultural *story/life/style*.
8. The *party life/night action/nightlife* in Rio de Janeiro is fantastic.
9. Hong Kong is becoming increasingly *unspoiled/diverse/varied*.
10. The best thing about Brazil is the sense of *liberty/freeing/freedom* as you walk around.

2 Add words or phrases from the box to complete the sentences. You will not use all of them.

recommend	to watch	to do	being
us to use	entering	afford	going
of watching	stand	to go	avoids
us using	to pass	urge	is
us to enter	doing		

1. I'm thinking of to Costa Rica. What's the weather like in April?
2. Dave can't to take a vacation, so he's camping in his yard this year!
3. Can you imagine an astronaut? You could go into space!
4. Mario's so lazy: he always doing the dishes.
5. I tried to persuade Gail a DVD tonight, but she didn't want to.
6. I can't smoking; cigarette smoke makes me sick.
7. They advised traveler's checks because they're safer.
8. My teachers always encouraged me my best.
9. Libby urged the competition. She was right: we won!

3 To complete the comparisons in the article, add six more words.

> The online community is predicting that blogs will soon replace print journalism. While publishing material on the web is far easier *than* getting it into print, I have my doubts about this prediction. First, blogs are considerably reliable than print journalism. There are checks and balances for print journalists, and newspapers are far likely than websites to be prosecuted if they get the facts wrong. Reading a blog is almost the same reading a diary; if it is full of lies and exaggeration, there's not a lot you can do. The advantage of blogs is that they are personal and usually unedited. But more we rely on them for news, the less sure we can be that we are getting the full story. Basically, they act as a voice that cannot be silenced. The easier the web becomes to use, more diverse voices it will contain, and that's a great thing. As for me, I'm far comfortable getting my news from a newspaper!

4 Put the letters in parentheses in the correct order to complete the article.

The town where I grew up used to be a beautiful, ________ (**1.** usnpilode) little place. It was a ________ (**2.** ntrauiql), sleepy kind of town, and that's how I liked it. It was ________ (**3.** fof hte eabtne rtakc), surrounded by rolling hills and a ________ (**4.** nimaficnget) forest. I went back recently and was surprised at how much it had changed. For one thing, a new shopping mall had been built right near the center of town. I went inside, and it was ________ (**5.** apkdec) with shoppers. Then I drove to my old school, which was still ________ (**6.** gutibsln) with children, though the building looked a little ________ (**7.** nru-nwod). I went in, hoping to see some of my old teachers, but a security guard promptly kicked me out. So I drove toward the forest, assuming that some things would remain unchanged. Unfortunately, the forest didn't exist any more; they'd built a ________ (**8.** asvt) apartment complex there.

5 Do the pairs of sentences have similar (*S*) or different (*D*) meanings?

____ **1. a.** It's almost the same price whether you buy your ticket on the Internet or at the station.
b. Buying the ticket on the Internet is a little bit cheaper, but there's hardly any difference.

____ **2. a.** I'd rather live in a quiet community than one with lots of nightlife.
b. In my view, the more nightlife, the better.

____ **3. a.** The less we mix with that community, the less trouble we'll have.
b. We're much better off mixing with that community.

____ **4. a.** Togo is not nearly as expensive as South Africa.
b. South Africa is considerably more expensive than Togo.

____ **5. a.** Lugano is a little prettier than my home town.
b. My home town isn't quite as pretty as Lugano.

____ **6. a.** Busan is not nearly as exciting as the town where I grew up.
b. Busan is far more exciting than the town where I grew up.

6 Complete the crossword.

Across

3. I ____ you to visit the Vatican Museum while in Rome. You shouldn't miss it.

5. If you go to Panama City, ____ out for pickpockets.

8. Everyone said the movie was great, but I thought it was a little ____.

Down

1. The drinks are ____ in this nightclub. They shouldn't be this expensive!

2. You can't miss the Picasso exhibition! It's a ____.

4. The restaurant is not fancy, but its food is tasty and you get a great ____ for the money.

6. That statue isn't all it's ____ up to be. I thought it would be much more beautiful than it is.

7. You should watch ____ for the mosquitoes. There are a lot of them at this time of year.

UNIT 3
Stories

LESSON 1

Reading

1a Read the title of the article. What do you think the article will be about? Circle your choice.

a. Some communities claim they have a secret way to stay young and healthy. The article describes how they manage to do it.

b. Some communities claim that many of their people live until they are over a hundred. The article disputes these claims.

c. Some researchers believe that ancient communities are healthier than modern societies. The article lists the problems of modern living.

b Read the article to check your answer.

c Read the article again. On a separate sheet of paper, write questions for these answers.

1. It was an academic paper about the people he studied.
2. A local man whose stated age changed by eleven years in only four years.
3. It was lost when a church caught fire.
4. Because in these societies, the older you are, the more respected you are.
5. The condition of the people's bones, and official documents.
6. Because they were afraid of being caught.

The old age hoax

A little old man walks the fields of Vilcabamba, Ecuador. His skin is wrinkled from exposure to the sun, and his legs move slowly, steadily. As the sky turns red, he puts down his ancient tools and walks across the valley to the mud hut that he calls home. He is 140 years old.

Hard to believe? Well, Methuselah lived to be 969, according to the Bible. And, according to some, there are communities – the people of Vilcabamba, the Abkhazians of Georgia, the Hunza of Pakistan – that contain large numbers of centenarians, those lucky people who live to be 100.

Let's take a trip back in time. January,1973. Dr. Alexander Leaf, of Harvard University, publishes a report in *National Geographic* magazine that describes his journeys to study the Hunza, Abkhazians, and the Vilcabambas. He calls his report *Every Day Over 100 is a Gift.* According to Leaf, there are ten times the number of centenarians found in these areas than is normal in modern Western civilizations. The article causes a minor stir in anthropology circles and one or two commercial ones too: an American entrepreneur makes plans to invest in bottled water from Vilcabamba, and a Japanese company discusses building a hotel there for elderly tourists.

But then, as further studies followed Leaf's, the evidence began to point not to mythical communities with ancient youth-preserving lifestyles, but rather to lies, exaggeration, and the creation of a sensational myth. Although Leaf's report sounded plausible enough at first, a number of questions arose later. When Dr. Leaf returned to Vilcabamba four years after his first visit, one of the villagers, Miguel Carpiro, had miraculously become eleven years older. Leaf asked to see Carpiro's birth certificate, but was told that it had been destroyed in a church fire.

Indeed, birth records were one of the main problems; societies with low levels of literacy usually don't have them. And, in Vilcabamba, names were used repeatedly within the family, so that grandfathers, fathers, and sons might have exactly the same name, adding to the confusion. Furthermore, old age is revered in societies such as Abkhazian, and so people exaggerate to improve their social status. When the exaggeration also brings about increased attention and tourism, there is even further temptation to add a few years to your age.

After Leaf's report, two researchers, Mazess and Forman, went to Vilcabamba and checked skeletal conditions, as well as existing records. They found enormous inaccuracies everywhere. Miguel Carpiro, who had claimed to be 121, was actually 87. His mother was born five years after he'd claimed to be born! Another researcher, a Russian geneticist named Zhores Medvedev, studied the people of Abkhazia, who had also claimed to have many centenarians. He discovered that many of them had assumed the identities of their parents. Some of these people were World War I deserters, and they had used their dead parents' names in order to avoid detection.

So, myth or reality? We don't know for sure. Roger Maupin, an anthropologist, says of these people: "Their lifestyle is certainly healthy. They have constant steady work, a good diet, and a small community untroubled by such things as war, technology, and the stresses these bring. But we just have no reliable evidence about their real age. Ultimately, I don't think it matters. It's not the age you live to; it's the quality of your life that counts."

d Underline words or phrases in the article that mean:

1. people who are still alive at 100 (*n.*) (line 10)
2. attract a lot of attention (*v.*) (lines 17–18)
3. believable (*adj.*) (line 26)
4. deeply respected (*adj.*) (line 37)
5. importance (how much a person is respected) within a community (*n.*) (line 39)
6. causes (*v.*) (lines 39–40)
7. soldiers who run away from battle (*n.*) (line 51)
8. being found (*v.*) (line 52)

Grammar

2 Complete each sentence using the correct form of the verb in parentheses.

1. Who ______________ to on the phone when I came home? (talk)
2. We could tell from his filthy clothes that he ______________ in the garden for hours. (work)
3. I knew something was wrong because the dog ______________ constantly. (bark)
4. Once I ______________ her, I knew she was the girl for me. (meet)
5. The maid obviously hadn't come because my room ______________. (clean)
6. ______________ of him before you saw the movie? (hear)
7. Later, I realized that we ______________ about different people! (talk)
8. I couldn't pick him up because my car ______________. (fix)

3 Circle the sentence that describes each picture.

1. **a.** At midnight, when we got back, she had already put the baby to bed.
   b. At midnight, when we got back, she was putting the baby to bed.
2. **a.** The game was canceled because it had been snowing.
   b. The game was canceled because it was snowing.
3. **a.** Jim had painted the bathroom.
   b. Jim had been painting the bathroom.
4. **a.** I got home and discovered that my apartment had been broken into.
   b. I got home and discovered that my apartment was being broken into.
5. **a.** Junichi told us he had been training for the Olympics.
   b. Junichi told us he was training for the Olympics.
6. **a.** When I saw Joan, she was going to the salon.
   b. When I saw Joan, she had been to the salon.

Reading

1a Read the short story on the right. Answer the questions on a separate sheet of paper.

1. Who do you think had the idea to go birdwatching?
2. What type of town do Thomas and Rosie live in?
3. Is Thomas good at spelling? How do we know?
4. What type of person is Rosie? How do we know?
5. What does the father think of Thomas's description of the birdwatching trip?
6. Why was Rosie "disgraced"?
7. How does the father feel about his children?
8. Which of these words would you use to describe the story? Circle one or more words.

   surprising *surreal* *traditional*
   shocking *funny*

b Find words in the story that mean:

1. ready and waiting (*adj.*) (line 9) ____________
2. high-pitched shout (*n.*) (line 20) ____________
3. walking with short steps, body moving from side to side (*v.*) (line 32) ____________
4. walking vigorously (usually through something) (*v.*) (line 34) ____________
5. preserved in some kind of (solid) form, but no longer living, growing, or used (*adj.*) (line 35) ____________
6. thrown away or abandoned (*adj.*) (line 41) ____________
7. made something uneven or messy by rubbing it (*v.*) (line 42) ____________
8. looking at something, angrily (*v.*) (line 48) ____________

c Find the object or person in the story that these words refer to.

1. it (line 4) ____________
2. on which (line 10) ____________
3. this same sound (line 25) ____________
4. it (line 27) ____________
5. It (line 30) ____________
6. it (line 33) ____________
7. he (line 46) ____________
8. its (line 48) ____________

Birdwatcher

At 2:32 on the afternoon of July 10, eight-year-old Thomas Smith saw a large yellow-beaked eagle rise from the roof of the local post office. His sister, ten-year-old Rosie, didn't see it because she was busy applying her mother's lipstick to her small, but very pretty, mouth, and in any case, she wasn't all that excited about birdwatching.

"Rosie," said Thomas. "How do you spell eagle?" His pencil was poised above a notebook that had a picture of an owl on the front and on which Thomas had written "BuRds". B-u-r-d-s.

"Eagle?" said Rosie. "I-d-i-o-t."

"Very funny."

"E-e-g-l-e."

Thomas wrote it down. Eegle. 2:32, July 10. Franklin Road Post Office.

They crossed the street, slipping between the fat cars all stopped still in the summer heat, fingers tapping outside windows. It was at this point that Thomas heard the distant shriek of seagulls and recognized the sound at once. The previous summer, they had spent a week with their parents at a beach town eating huge sausages in pools of grease and getting red-faced in the sun, and had been woken every morning by this same sound.

"Rosie, how do you spell seagull?"

"Same as eagle, but it starts with an s."

At 2:58, Thomas and Rosie paused for a minute while Rosie searched her purse for the blue eye shadow that she had removed from her mother's drawer. It was called Aquamarine Dream. At this moment, Thomas noticed a penguin waddling down Main Street. Thomas watched it go by, the penguin merrily traipsing through the cigarette butts and chewing gum stains fossilized on the sidewalk, and Thomas wrote "Pen Win" in his notebook.

Later, while the disgraced Rosie was grounded in her room, her mother's makeup returned, Thomas sat at his father's feet and explained about the eagle on the post office roof, the ostrich outside the library, and the vulture in Rosemary Gardens snacking on a discarded bag of popcorn. His father ruffled the boy's hair, laughed to himself, and thought about the wonders of the child's imagination. And the man felt at peace with the world and with his two naughty children, at least until 3:11 A.M. the following morning, when he was woken by an enormous white swan sitting at the end of his bed, its yellow eyes glaring.

Vocabulary

2 Complete the book review using words from the box.

one-dimensional	hooked	turner	base
best-seller	gripping	down	true
bookworm	depicts	found	avid

Meredith Johnson's new book, *Feather Man*, like her four previous novels, is a page-__________ (1.) and destined to be a __________ (2.). Unusually for Johnson, she doesn't __________ (3.) her plot on a true story (her last book was based on the __________ (4.) story of a failed bank robbery), though once again she brilliantly __________ (5.) Edinburgh's criminal underworld, where a wrong word can earn you a slashing with a razor blade, and a wrong move can get you injected with something even worse.

She soon has the reader __________ (6.). The hero, Paul Schroeder, detective and __________ (7.), who spends half his life in a library, finds himself investigating a writer called Max Dowling, when Schroeder realizes that Dowling leaves clues to unsolved crimes in his books.

I __________ (8.) the story totally __________ (9.), and if the characters are a little __________ (10.)—for example, an unrealistic group of criminals all seem to wear leather jackets, smoke a lot, and have frightening pets—the pace and action more than make up for it. Frankly, I couldn't put *Feather Man* __________ (11.). I recommend it highly, not only for __________ (12.) readers of Johnson's work, but for new converts, too.

3 Read what these people say about their partners. Circle the correct choice.

1. She comes *across/over/around* as very kind and gentle when you first meet her.
2. Once you *become to know/get to know/seem to know* her, you realize she's really funny.
3. The thing that *strikes/hits you/strikes you* about Tyler is that he's so intelligent.
4. What I really *think about/like for/like about* Karen is her sense of humor.
5. Matthew is *such a/so/a such* talented guy that you have to admire him.
6. He can be *a bit of/a bit/bit* mean sometimes, especially when he's in a bad mood.

4a Match the beginning of each compound adjective with its end.

____ 1. single-	a. minded
____ 2. self-	b. minded
____ 3. thick-	c. offish
____ 4. kind-	d. oriented
____ 5. stand-	e. hearted
____ 6. career-	f. skinned
____ 7. level-	g. sufficient
____ 8. absent-	h. headed

b Match the compound adjectives in Exercise 4a to the people in these paragraphs. You may match more than one to each person. Two compound adjectives are not used.

1. Bradbury was determined to claw his way to the top of the company, trampling on whoever got in his way. He had been in the business only six months when he decided that the quickest way to get promoted would be to murder William DeFries.

   ____

2. Delilah sat in the corner for the whole party. Whenever a young man approached, she immediately feigned boredom and continued sipping from her slim glass of ice-water, eyes raised to the ceiling.

   ____

3. My mother was the type of person who regularly left home in her slippers. She frequently forgot to turn off ovens, lights, televisions, and radios. She was known to make phone calls and, on being answered, immediately forget not only why she was calling, but who she was calling.

   ____

4. Being short, skinny, and ugly, I have been called names since I was old enough to walk. "Stick insect, creepy-crawly, witch, rat-face, alien, ET, lizard." I answer the name-callers with a wink and a smile. You see, I just don't care.

   ____

5. Mr. Trimble had watery gray eyes and a pocket permanently stuffed full of sweets for any children he came across. He walked with the slowness of a snail, leaving no slime, but a trail of happiness wherever he went.

   ____

LESSON 3

Reading

1a Read three jokes and match the pictures to the jokes.

A

B

C

____ **1. Liar, Liar**

A policeman stops a car because it is speeding. He asks the driver for his license. "I don't have one," says the driver. "And the car's not mine. I stole it. But I think I saw a driver's license in the glove box when I put my gun in there."

"You stole it?! You have a gun in the glove box?!"

"Yes," says the driver. "I put it there just before I threw the car owner's body in the trunk." The policeman calls for backup, and five minutes later, four police cars arrive. The captain says, "Sir, may I see your license?"

"Sure," says the driver. He opens the glove box slowly and gives him the license. The police captain says, "So, no gun in the glove box?"

"Gun? Of course not!"

"And no body in the trunk?"

"What?!" says the driver. And the captain says: "My police officer told me you had a gun in the glove box and a body in the trunk."

"Yeah, and I bet the liar told you I was speeding too."

____ **2. The Cat Who Came Back**

A couple owned a cat, but the man hated it. So one day he decided to get rid of it. He drove ten blocks and threw the cat out of the car window. But when he got home, there the cat was, lying on the doormat. So the next day, he drove twenty blocks and threw the cat into a river. But, on entering his driveway, the cat was there again, fast asleep by the door. So the next day he drove fifteen blocks, took a left, took a right, went down the highway, crossed a couple of bridges, and threw the cat into a large hole in the ground. After driving a while, he called his wife. "Is the cat there?" he asked.

"Yes," she said. "Why do you ask?"

"OK, put the cat on the phone. I'm lost and I need directions home."

____ **3. Some Good Advice**

A new manager walks into his office and finds four numbered envelopes on the desk. Number one says "Open me first." So he opens it, and finds a letter from the previous manager. It says, "When the company is having problems and you don't know what to do, open these envelopes in order." So he puts the envelopes away and forgets about them. Six months later, the company is in big trouble and the manager may lose his job. Suddenly, he remembers the envelopes, so he opens the second envelope. In it there is a message that says, "Blame everything on me, the previous manager." He does this and saves his job, and the company recovers. But, six months after this, the company is in trouble again and losing money fast. He opens the third envelope and reads the message. It says, "Blame everything on the government." He does this, and everyone agrees, and he keeps his job. Six months later, the company is in even bigger trouble, and the workers are on strike. So he opens the fourth envelope. The message says: "Prepare four envelopes."

b Complete the sentences.

Joke 1

1. The driver was stopped because he was ____________.
2. There wasn't a gun in the ____________ or a body in the ____________.

Joke 2

3. A man wanted to ____________ of a cat.
4. The man needed ____________ to get home.

Joke 3

5. The second note said, "____________ everything on me."
6. The manager's final problem was that the workers were on ____________.

c Read the sentences below. Mark the sentences that are probably sarcastic (*SA*), show surprise (*S*), and those that are said calmly (*C*).

____ 1. "You stole it?! You have a gun in the glove box?!"

____ 2. "I put it there just before I threw the car owner's body into the trunk."

____ 3. "Sir, may I see your license?"

____ 4. "So, no gun in the glove box?"

____ 5. "Gun? Of course not!"

____ 6. "My police officer told me you had a gun in the glove box and a body in the trunk."

____ 7. "Yeah, and I bet the liar told you I was speeding, too."

Grammar

2 Complete each story with the participle or gerund of verbs from the box.

have/catch	ask	play
celebrate	call	cheat

In the wild old days of cowboys and saloons, __________ (1.) at cards was likely to get you killed. __________ (2.) cheating in a saloon in 1857, Donald Blewett was shot dead. The men __________ (3.) still wanted to finish their game, however, and they needed another player, so they asked a stranger to join them. This stranger then proceeded to win over $4,000. __________ (4.) to the scene a while later, the police decided to try and find Donald Blewett's nearest relative. After __________ (5.) around to find out the dead man's name, they discovered that the stranger __________ (6.) his $4,000 jackpot was Blewett's son, who hadn't seen his father for over ten years.

have/place	tell	involve
have/make	bet	know

__________ (7.) should never have been easier. __________ (8.) elaborate plans to cheat, horse owner and politician Horatio Ortiz placed "the perfect bet" on a horse race in Argentina. He owned all six of the horses __________ (9.) in the race, and he employed the six English jockeys. After __________ (10.) the jockeys the order in which they should finish, Ortiz thought he couldn't lose. However, __________ (11.) his bet, he got a surprise. Halfway through the race, a thick fog descended on the course. As a result, the race was declared null and void, with no winner. Ortiz, __________ (12.) for his money-making ability, lost a fortune.

3 Six of these sentences contain mistakes. Check the correct sentences. Correct the mistakes in the others.

____ 1. Not having heard the music, I can't really judge it.

____ 2. On been arrested by the police, Teresa admitted that she was guilty of fraud.

____ 3. She broke her leg while to play hockey.

____ 4. He stood there in front of us, desolate, robbed of everything he'd ever owned.

____ 5. To help other people wasn't something that usually made Mrs. Davies happy.

____ 6. Having been given the car just the day before, Lucas promptly crashed it.

____ 7. All of the boys, hoped to be basketball stars, trained for six hours every day.

____ 8. Told by his teacher that he had the ability to pass his exam, Kenzo finally achieved his goal.

____ 9. Having wake up at 4:00 A.M., we were exhausted by 11:00.

____ 10. After being listening to the speech for four hours, Bianca eventually fell asleep.

Vocabulary

4 Complete the crossword.

Across

1. comic drama using unlikely situations and people acting stupidly
2. a funny drawing
3. make something or someone seem ridiculous (often in order to laugh at people who have power)
4. comic moments connected to very serious subjects

Down

3. humor based on extremely strange connections
5. giving the impression that something is greater or larger than it really is
6. humorous use of words that sound the same but have different meanings
7. when you say the opposite of what you mean, for a humorous effect

Review

1 Complete the crossword.

Across

1. A person who forgets little things is ____-minded.
4. A person who is difficult to talk to and not very friendly is stand-____.
6. A person who is determined to do something is single-____.
7. A person who is always thinking about how to get further in his or her career is career-____.
8. A person who is very calm, even when in a tricky situation, is level-____.

Down

2. A person who can look after himself without help is self-____.
3. A person who doesn't get offended easily when criticized is thick-____.
5. A person who is generous and nice to others is kind-____.

2 Circle the correct word or phrase.

1. In order to avoid hurting people, I think it's OK to tell ____.
   a. a feeble excuse b. a white lie c. a rumor
2. Advertising writers aren't exactly liars, but they tend to slightly ____.
   a. exaggerate b. gossip c. tell lies
3. We heard the fire alarm, but it turned out to be a ____.
   a. rumor b. false c. hoax
4. My mother is the best ____ I know.
   a. bookworm b. storyteller c. story
5. Are you good at telling ____?
   a. storytellers b. jokes c. hoaxes

3 Complete the sentences using the correct form of verbs from the box.

memorize	drive	face
turn into	write	make
get up	leave	read

1. By midday I was really tired, because I ____________ on the freeway since 5 A.M.
2. She said all the noise was because the building next door ____________ a shopping mall. The work wouldn't be completed until the following May.
3. They desperately wanted to see Francesca, but the janitor told them that she ____________ already.
4. One of the children recited the whole story. Apparently, he ____________ it for weeks.
5. When I got home, the fridge ____________ a weird noise, so I called the repairman.
6. He ____________ his autobiography in the months before he died, so although it wasn't finished, we had a good idea of his life story.
7. My friends knew the movie had a twist in the end, but I didn't because I ____________ the book.
8. Rob tried to take a photo of Lily, but she ____________ the wrong way.
9. ____________ you ____________ early this morning? I thought I heard you.

4 Correct the sentences by adding or crossing out one word.

1. You're such fast swimmer; I could never keep up with you.
2. What one thing I don't like about Samantha is that she's so selfish.
3. The thing strikes you about Tami is her determination.
4. He can be a bit of annoying sometimes, but his heart's in the right place.
5. Once you get to know of Maurice, you'll like him.

5 Circle the correct choice. More than one answer may be possible.

1. _To hope/Hoping/Hoped_ to find a new wife, James settled in San Francisco.
2. _Restored/Having been restored/After restored_ to its former glory, the painting was re-hung.
3. _Ran/To run/Running_ marathons is what she does best.
4. I know the man _having sat/sat/sitting_ in the blue car.
5. _While driving/Driven/Having driven_ in the tunnel, keep your lights on.
6. _On hearing/Heard/Having heard_ the news, he rushed over to the hospital.
7. _Buried/Being buried/Burying_ in the cemetery is a famous scientist of the early twentieth century.
8. _After catching/After being caught/Having been caught_, the robber put down his gun.
9. The photos _taken/being taken/having been taken_ today will turn out fine. The light is perfect.
10. _After being treated/Treating/Treated_ by experts, the dog began to recover.

6 Match the descriptions to types of humor from the box. Two are not used.

black humor	cartoons	farce
surreal humor	irony	puns
exaggeration	satire	

1. Comedian John Weeding spent an hour of his great show doing impressions of President Obama and other politicians, and the audience lapped up his hilarious take on modern society. ________
2. We see the usual tricks of the genre in this tedious play: mistresses hiding in wardrobes, husbands caught with their pants down, and a plot that goes from the silly to the ridiculous. ________
3. Why is a bad joke like a broken pencil? It has no point. If you like this type of humor—and most children do—*The Bumper Book of Kids' Jokes* is for you. ________
4. He goes way beyond what you usually find in the back pages of the newspaper. The writing and drawing are so exquisite that he's been called a mix between Leonardo and Woody Allen. ________
5. Her whole act is based on creating bizarre combinations. At one point, she compares a chocolate cake to the history of space flight, and after the intermission she emerges wearing a lobster on her head. ________
6. The entire play revolves around a search for a dead body. Somehow, Luke Williams manages to wring humor out of a very dark situation. ________

UNIT 4

Moving forward

LESSON 1

Vocabulary

1a Match the words to their common collocations.

___ 1. serious	a. gravity
___ 2. special	b. technology
___ 3. foreseeable	c. injury
___ 4. computer	d. future
___ 5. genetic	e. engineering
___ 6. latest	f. nerd
___ 7. defy	g. power

b Complete the sentences with collocations from Exercise 1a.

1. If your laptop is broken, talk to John. He's such a ______________ that it'll be easy for him to fix.
2. She likes to have all the ______________. Her electronic devices are never out of date.
3. In the future, scientists may be able to use ______________ to detect and stop diseases before they become harmful.
4. In the ______________, all cars may be controlled by computer technology, rather than human drivers.
5. Although the cars were damaged in the accident, there were no ______________ or deaths.
6. I think everyone dreams of being able to ______________ and fly.
7. He looked like a normal man, but he had a ______________: he was incredibly strong.

Reading

2 Read the article and choose the best title. ___

a. Superheroes—too strong for their own good?
b. Real-life superheroes—inspiration for developing superhero characters
c. Making a superhero—fact or fiction?

From gamma-radiation to radioactive spiders, superheroes are born in a variety of weird and wonderful ways. But how realistic are they?

Being born on other planets, or finding cosmic lanterns, requires a huge leap of the imagination. But what about the humans who develop special powers by slightly more prosaic means—how plausible are they?

Take The Incredible Hulk: Scientist Dr. Robert Banner receives a huge dose of gamma rays while working on a nuclear bomb. Gamma rays are real enough, being produced by nuclear explosions, but the bad news is that the gamma-radiation that gave Robert Banner his powers would only have caused fatal radiation sickness in real life.

Forgetting that minor point, Lois Gresh, author of *Science and Superheroes*, argues it's just about possible to create a believable version of The Hulk. Banner could take large amounts of (highly dangerous) anabolic steroids to produce that pumped-up look, which in real life could cause his notorious rages, as they increase aggressive mood swings. As for the green skin, French genetic researchers have at least created a glowing green rabbit by genetic engineering, using fluorescent protein.

Spider-Man, on the other hand, has bigger problems. While a radioactive spider could exist (spiders are tolerant to radiation), an animal does not transfer DNA via a bite. And even if it did, it couldn't fuse with our DNA. If being ingested were enough to make this happen, we'd get characteristics of, say, apples or chickens whenever we ate them.

Batman—the "Dark Knight"—might be the most realistic of the heroes, says Gresh. It is, of course, possible for a person to train obsessively in martial arts and subjects such as criminology. But in this case, it's gadgets that make Batman who he is. Most of Batman's toys, from his tiny cameras, to smoke grenades, to superstrong ropes, exist in the 21st century. Even creating a batmobile shouldn't present modern carmakers with too much difficulty.

Grammar

3 On a separate sheet of paper, write sentences about the article using the words in parentheses.

Ex: I . . . you would find a cosmic lantern. (whether)
I doubt whether you would find a cosmic lantern.

1. Gamma rays . . . produced by nuclear explosions. (definitely)
2. It's . . . that if Dr. Banner had received this radiation, he would have died. (likely)
3. There . . . we could create a believable version of The Hulk in reality. (slight)
4. Giving him anabolic steroids would . . . create his pumped-up look. (almost)
5. These . . . cause him to become more aggressive and moody. (might)
6. There . . . that we could create green skin by genetic engineering. (remote)
7. A radioactive spider . . . exist. (conceivably)
8. An animal . . . of transferring DNA via a bite. (stands)
9. If it did transfer its DNA, it wouldn't . . . of fusing with our DNA. (chance)
10. If ingesting DNA were enough to change our own DNA, we . . . adopt the characteristics of chickens and apples when we ate them. (presumably)
11. Batman . . . be the most realistic of the heroes. (well)
12. There . . . that modern carmakers could even create a batmobile. (distinct)

4 Complete the sentences with words from the box.

conceivably	against	doubt	well
likelihood	doubtful	slight	any
possibility	chances	bound	stand

1. **A:** Do you think there's __________ chance that we'll see Martha this weekend?
   B: I wouldn't count on it, but there's a __________ chance that she'll show up.
2. The odds are __________ us meeting the sales targets for this quarter, but there's a strong __________ that things will improve over the coming months.
3. Rooney doesn't __________ a chance of being chosen for the team.
4. I __________ whether they'll finish the work by the end of the week.
5. We may __________ have the chance to explore the area in more detail later.
6. Why did you do that? It's __________ to upset her.
7. It's __________ that they could have chosen a worse time to announce the news.
8. It could __________ help us in the future.
9. There's every __________ that he will resign soon.
10. The __________ are that we'll beat them in the Cup Final.

Reading

5 Read the news story. Then answer the questions on a separate sheet of paper.

Real-life Superheroes

Leisa Hodgkinson is a small woman, but she lifted a one-ton car off a seven-year-old boy trapped underneath. The boy was severely injured but has since recovered completely and now calls Leisa "Wonder Woman." She said at the time that she found the strength to lift the car after thinking of her own son, who was the same age as the trapped boy.

Miami man Tony Santores won an award from the mayor for outstanding bravery in 2000, after helping to rescue a mother and child from a burning building in a daring climb worthy of Spider-Man. He scaled the front of the building, despite minimal hand and foot-holds, and stayed in the smoke-filled room with the two to comfort them until the fire-fighters arrived.

1. Why does the young boy call Leisa "Wonder Woman"?
2. Why did Tony Santores climb up the side of the building?

LESSON 2

Vocabulary

1 Circle the correct word to complete each sentence.

1. What are you ____ to later? We're going out for a meal.
   a. up b. in c. on
2. Do you have anything ____ up for tonight?
   a. straight b. going c. lined
3. We *were* planning to all meet for lunch next week, but the plans have fallen ____.
   a. off b. out c. through
4. Unfortunately, I'm ____ up all week figuring out the accounts.
   a. tied b. turned c. lined
5. Please try and come. Can't you ____ out of going to see your grandmother?
   a. go b. come c. get
6. They called ____ the wedding because she's changed her mind.
   a. on b. of c. off
7. I'll let you know if anything else comes ____.
   a. up b. on c. in
8. Do you know if the meeting is still ____?
   a. for b. on c. in

2 Match the beginning of the sentence to its end.

____ 1. She's more or
____ 2. I was kind of hoping
____ 3. I only see them once in a
____ 4. We work mainly with textiles and
____ 5. We'll be arriving at
____ 6. We were sort
____ 7. We go camping from

a. while.
b. about five-ish.
c. less finished redecorating.
d. of expecting to hear from you.
e. you could help.
f. time to time.
g. that kind of thing.

Grammar

3 Circle the correct choice.

1. *I'll/I'm going to* pick you up from the airport if you want.
2. I have a doctor's appointment this afternoon, so *I'm leaving/I leave* work at 3 P.M.
3. What sort of job do you think you *will do/will be doing* in ten years?
4. By the time we get there, all the food *will be/will have been* eaten.
5. I'm sure you'll have a great time wherever *you decide/you'll decide* to go.
6. He asked if we *will/would* take this case for him.
7. The reception is bad in here. I'*ll/'m going to* call you back in a minute.
8. He's not coming until Thursday, and we*'ll be finishing/'ll have finished* by then.
9. The flight *leaves/is going to leave* at 9:20.

Reading

The "Slow movement"

(1) Carl Honoré, a recovered "speedaholic," had an epiphany that caused him to slow down the hectic pace of his life. A journalist based in London, Honoré read a newspaper article on time-saving tips that referenced a book of one-minute bedtime stories. He found it an appealing idea, since he'd already developed the habit of speed-reading stories to his son. "My first reaction was, yes, one-minute bedtime stories," he said. "My next thought was, whoa, has it really come to this? That was really when a light bulb went off in my head."

(2) He realized he had become so anxious to rush through the nightly ritual that he was reading seven or even eight stories in less time than he'd normally spend reading one. He wasn't making the most of this quality time.

(3) So, he embarked on finding a way to address the issue of "time poverty," the constant fast-forward motion in which many overscheduled, stressed-out people are always rushing toward their next task—work, meals, family time—rather than savoring what they consider most important.

(4) Honoré's book, *In Praise of Slowness: How a Worldwide Movement Is Challenging the Cult of Speed*, has made him the unofficial godfather of a growing cultural shift toward slowing down. "[There's a] backlash against the mainstream dictate that faster is always better, which puts quantity always ahead of quality," he said. "People all across the West are waking up to the folly of that."

(5) For advocates of the Slow Movement, it's not about rejecting technology or changing modern life completely, but rather about keeping it all in balance—not talking on the phone, driving, and checking email while headed to the drive-thru before the next meeting.

"I love technology. I love speed. You need some things to be fast—hockey . . ., a fast Internet connection," Honoré said. "But," he said, "my passion for speed had become an addiction. I was doing everything faster."

(6) What to Do?

To make the transition to a slower life, Honoré has several suggestions: don't schedule something in every free moment of your day—prioritize activities and cut from the bottom of the list; limit television watching; and keep an eye on your "personal speedometer" so you can gauge when you are rushing for speed's sake rather than necessity.

(7) But don't expect the change to happen immediately—or even naturally. "You don't slow down by snapping your fingers, "Now I'm slow," said Honoré, who got a speeding ticket on his way to a Slow Food dinner as he researched the book. "That happens," he said. "My life has been transformed by it, but I still feel that old itch."

4a Read the article. Mark the statements true (*T*) or false (*F*).

____ **1.** Carl Honoré came to a slow realization that he was living life too fast.

____ **2.** He was reading an article about ways to spend more quality time with your children.

____ **3.** Carl initially thought that one-minute bedtime stories were a good idea, since he regularly read stories to his son.

____ **4.** He reflected that he needed to readdress the priorities in his life.

____ **5.** According to the article, people are stressed because they fail to think ahead to the next task.

____ **6.** Carl believes that people are starting to question whether quality is better than quantity.

____ **7.** People who join the Slow Movement do not use computers, travel in cars, or watch television.

____ **8.** His advice is to reduce the number of things you do by deciding what is least important.

b Underline words or phrases in the article that mean:

1. desperate (to do something) (*adj.*) (paragraph 2)
2. began (something long and difficult) (*v.*) (paragraph 3)
3. enjoying (*v.*) (paragraph 3)
4. a strong negative reaction (*adj.*) (paragraph 4)
5. to measure (*v.*) (paragraph 6)
6. a desire to do something you should not (*n.*) (paragraph 7)

c Complete the sentences using words or phrases from Exercise 4b.

1. We ____________ on a long, difficult journey.
2. I'm ____________ to speak to Phyllis before she leaves.
3. Try to ____________ the views while you are here. We might never come back.
4. It was hard to ____________ his reaction to the new ideas.
5. There has been a strong ____________ to the changes.

LESSON 3

Vocabulary

1 Complete each sentence by putting the letters in parentheses in the correct order.

1. There is a lot of pressure, and the job is very __________. (niegmdand)
2. She is a naturally __________ piano player. (fitegd)
3. The teenagers in the area are thugs in the __________. (kanimg)
4. Mozart was a musical __________. (dipogry)
5. The movie star was the subject of much __________ from his fans. (donulatai)
6. Staff members are trained by their ______. (srepe)
7. People who dye their hair strange colors used to be considered ______. (karsef)

Reading

2 Read the article. Make a list of Kishan's interests and achievements on a separate sheet of paper.

Nine-year-old calls the shots

1 The director is barking orders from the edit suite as he cuts a shot featuring Jackie Shroff, a leading Indian movie star. It could be an everyday scene in Bollywood—except the director is a nine-year-old boy.

2 Master Kishan, as he is known, has already been in 24 movies and appeared in more than 1,000 episodes of a popular television soap opera. He is now fulfilling another dream: becoming the youngest director not just in India, but in the world. "I am different from other children, because this is the age for children to play," admitted Kishan, sitting in his director's seat, his feet not quite touching the floor. "I like playing, but not as much as other children. I don't know if the movie will be successful. I hope it will be. I have a good feeling about it."

3 Dressed in a black corduroy shirt and dark jeans, he looked like any other affluent middle-class Indian child. Later, at a local cafe, he ordered coffee and mysore pak, a buttery sweet pudding, while fielding approaches from admiring fans.

4 Kishan, whose favorite actors are Arnold Schwarzenegger and Amithabh Bachchan, a Bollywood superstar, began his acting career at age four, after his friends urged his parents to send him for an audition. He was given a part in *Goddess of the Village*, a fantasy adventure, before landing a leading role in *Papa Pandu*, a daily Bangalore soap. He wrote a hit song for a movie at the age of six, and has sung on others.

5 Kishan's father, Shri Kanth, a tax official, said his son had been obsessed with cameras since he was a toddler. "We noticed that when the camera was on him his behavior would improve," he said. "After he started working on the soap, the staff would complain that he asked too many questions about this shot and that shot."

6 Kishan's transition to director began after he talked to children selling newspapers beside a busy road in Bangalore. When he asked them why they were not at school, some replied that they were orphans, others that they would be beaten if they went home without any money. Kishan was so moved that he wrote a short story about his encounter. "I want them to go to school, and I hope the film encourages them to want to go," he said.

7 With the help of local journalists, he turned his story into a screenplay, *C/o Footpath*, about a Bangalore boy drugged by a woman who uses him as a prop to beg on the streets.

8 Ironically, Kishan's commitments mean that he has attended school for only ten days a month during filming. His secretary picks up class notes to help him keep up. Kishan, nevertheless, shows little sign of missing classes. He speaks good English and Kanada, the local language, and understands Hindi and Tamil.

9 Shri Kanth, however, worries that his son is missing childhood, and recently invited his friends to bring their children on a beach holiday, so that Kishan could play. He was surprised to see him building row after row of sand castles. "When I asked him why he was building them in rows, he held his hands up to make a frame, and said it was to give the shot depth," he said. A child psychologist friend has reassured him his son is fine.

3 Read the article again. Then answer the questions on a separate sheet of paper.

1. What makes Kishan different from other children his age?
2. How did Kishan become involved in acting?
3. What triggered Kishan's move toward becoming a director?
4. What inspired Kishan's short story?
5. What does he hope to achieve through the movie?
6. How does Kishan keep up with his school work?
7. Why does his father worry?

4 Find words or expressions in the article that mean:

1. shouting instructions (*v.*) (paragraph 1) ______________
2. wealthy (*adj.*) (paragraph 3) ______________
3. encouraged (*v.*) (paragraph 4) ________
4. think about something all the time (*v.*) (paragraph 5) ______________
5. be hit many times (*v.*) (paragraph 6) ________
6. feel a strong emotion (sad/sympathetic) (*adj.*) (paragraph 6) ______________
7. a meeting (*n.*) (paragraph 6) ______________
8. something you use to help achieve a special effect (theatrical) (*n.*) (paragraph 7) ________
9. not fall behind (with work/study) (*v.*) (paragraph 8) ______________
10. make someone feel calmer/less worried (*v.*) (paragraph 9) ______________

Grammar

5 Circle the correct choice.

1. No sooner *we had heard/had we heard* the news, than the police called to tell us what had happened.
2. *Not only did she/Not only she did* break the rules, but she also lied about her behavior.
3. Only when *everyone has arrived/has everyone arrived* can we begin the discussions.
4. Rarely *have I been/I have been* so upset about something.
5. *Not since I went/Since I didn't go* to college have I made so many new friends.
6. No way *I am going/am I going* to pay for their mistake!
7. *Only if/If only* we work night and day will we get the job finished on time.
8. No longer *you do need to/do you need to* stand in long lines at airports. You can check in yourself!
9. Only after she left *did I/I did* realize what had happened.
10. Not only *the service is great/is the service great*, but it's the cheapest hotel in the area.

6 Complete each sentence with the correct word or phrase.

1. ________ could be more exotic than these picturesque islands.
2. ________ recently have we begun to understand how the disease spreads.
3. Not ________ the organizer called me did I find out about the meeting.
4. No ________ had the plane taken off than they had to make an emergency landing.
5. ________ for one minute did I think I would win the competition.
6. ________ will you find such fantastic examples of the style.
7. Never ________ have we achieved such great sales.
8. ________ when she began to sing did we realize she had a special talent.
9. ________ if you have your bags checked will you be allowed through the entrance.
10. ________ again will I ride on an elephant!

UNIT 4
Review

1 Complete the crossword.

Across

3. I'll let you know if anything ____ up.
6. She has a dental ____ this morning, so she's driving to my house this afternoon.
8. I was wondering what you were ____ to over the weekend.
11. I won't be able to go to the movies on Friday. There's an office party that night and I can't ____ out of it.
12. I have to work overtime this month, so our plans to visit Vancouver have ____ through.

Down

1. If you go to Panama City, ____ out for pickpockets.
2. Her phone has no ____ where she's at, so she'll call me back later.
4. Do you have anything ____ up for tonight?
5. We're ____ to pick her up from the airport at 9:00.
7. I can't make it tomorrow. I'm a little ____ up.
9. Are our ____ to see a movie still on?
10. We've had to ____ off the trip because we are just too busy.

2 Put the words in the correct order to make sentences.

1. winning/the/are/series/against/odds/their/the
   ____
2. the/we/flight/well/her/on/may/see
   ____
3. the/later/it/are/will/chances/that/rain
   ____
4. it/we/everything/doubtful/will/that/is/finish/today
   ____
5. competition/is/that/there/a/beat/distinct/we'll/the/possibility
   ____
6. promotion/he'll/likelihood/is/every/get/there/that/the
   ____
7. that/idea/to/well/excellent/prove/may/be/an
   ____
8. there/could/catch/a/chance/is/train/that/we/slight/the/earlier
   ____

3 Complete these sentences about the future, using the correct form of the verbs in parentheses. There may be more than one possibility.

1. That's fine. I ______________ you next week to confirm the details. (call)
2. We ______________ all the work by February. (finish)
3. OK, the taxi ______________ to pick us up in half an hour. (come)
4. I have no idea what I __________ next year. (do)
5. Is Anna feeling OK? She looks like she ______________ sick. (be)
6. Let me help you. I ______________ this pile, and you deal with the rest. (take)
7. I have to leave at 5:00. I ______________ Michael to discuss the budget. (meet)
8. The traffic is awful. I'm worried I __________ late. (be)
9. It was really good to see you. Hopefully, I ______________ you again soon. (see)
10. I'm stuck at work and I don't know when I ______________ home. (get)

4 Seven of these sentences contain mistakes. Check the correct sentences. Correct the mistakes in others.

____ 1. Not only they apologized for the inconvenience, but they have refunded the money!

____ 2. No sooner do you ask her to do a job than she has done it.

____ 3. Only after did I repeatedly ask them did I manage to get a response.

____ 4. Not since 2005 there has been such a hot summer.

____ 5. Rarely do you find someone with such great talent.

____ 6. Never before we have been able to photograph these small creatures in such detail.

____ 7. Only if we keep looking we will ever find the solution.

____ 8. No way am I going to dress up as Superman!

____ 9. Nowhere it does say that we aren't allowed to use this room.

____ 10. Not for one minute did I thought I would have to clean the whole place.

5 Complete the conversations.

1. **A:** How often do you manage to see your grandmother?
   B: Once in a ____________.
2. **A:** How long do you think the meeting will last?
   B: Pretty ____________ all day.
3. **A:** Should we get started early?
   B: OK. How about about six-____________?
4. **A:** What does your new job involve?
   B: There is a lot of talking to clients and that ____________ of thing.
5. **A:** Let's split the bill.
   B: Actually, I was ____________ of hoping you could pay.
6. **A:** What time shall we meet?
   B: About eight or ____________.
7. **A:** How often do you go to the city?
   B: Only ____________ in a while.
8. **A:** When should we meet?
   B: In an hour or ____________.
9. **A:** Do you ever visit your home town?
   B: Yes. I go back every so ____________.
10. **A:** Does it snow here much?
    B: ____________ much all year.

UNIT 5
Making money

LESSON 1

Vocabulary

1 Complete the sentences by putting the letters in parentheses in the correct order.

1. He came into a ______________ when his father died. (netourf)
2. It is common to ______________ in the stores to bring the price down. (galgeh)
3. Those bankers make their fortunes betting on changes in the ______________ market. (ctoks)
4. Let me buy everyone a drink. I got a ______________ today! (saire)
5. The business is trying to attract ______________ families. (ghih-monice)
6. Her ideas are unique, so her work is absolutely ______________. (crisepels)
7. It doesn't affect our salary, because we're paid on ______________. (smocsimino)
8. They have done really well considering their last business went ______________. (knaptrub)

2 Match the beginning of each sentence to its end.

____ 1. It was important that the brothers had a good relationship, as they were
____ 2. They decided to buy their uncle
____ 3. You need to strike the
____ 4. It's time he rolled up his
____ 5. They hired a consultant to
____ 6. They kept their business and private affairs separate in order not to
____ 7. I come from a marketing
____ 8. It will be up to the new manager to execute the

a. sleeves and got on with what he has to do.
b. crunch the numbers.
c. 50-50 partners in the business.
d. jeopardize their friendship.
e. right balance between working hard and enjoying yourself.
f. strategy we decide on.
g. out of his share of the company.
h. background.

Grammar

3 On a separate sheet of paper, rewrite the sentences to increase the emphasis. Use the words in parentheses.

Ex: Inflation is making it increasingly difficult for young people to buy a home. (own)
Inflation is making it increasingly difficult for young people to buy their own home.

1. It isn't certain that giving aid is the best way to help poorer countries. (means)
2. Kandinsky abandoned his law studies in order to train as an artist in Munich. (even)
3. Marco Diacono planted the UK's first ever olive grove in 2006. He hoped that global warming would help the trees to survive. (It)
4. We went to the Pantanal, in Brazil, to enjoy the wildlife, but I got a shock when I found an eight-foot-long caiman outside my tent. (did)
5. I would suggest you stay along the coast near Amalfi. (need)

Reading

4a Read the story. Describe how it makes you feel.

____

____

My Missing Brother

While most people have lots of memories about their older siblings, my memories of my older brother are limited. Buck was 14 years older than me—that in itself set us apart in different generations and different worlds. Before he went to prison, I have only the faded memories of a young child. No matter how I try, it is difficult to recall what life was like with him before incarceration. I do remember riding on his shoulders at the county fair and how he showed me how to skip a stone across the river. But beyond that, my mind draws a blank. My strongest childhood memories are about visiting him with my parents at the penitentiary in Elmira, New York.

It was a long drive to get there, and when we arrived, we were never alone. Other families waited in line as the electronic prison gates opened and closed loudly behind us in a process that seemed to me to take forever. My parents had to sign in, get fingerprinted, and go through a pat down to make sure they weren't carrying anything in. The process made me very uncomfortable, and I would get very quiet and listen to the banging of metal and the echoes of voices in the cold, uninviting rooms.

They would take us to the visiting room where armed guards watched carefully as prisoners were brought in. My brother would saunter over with a smile on his face looking tall and handsome and in good health. He would sit on the other side of a stainless steel table, separated from us by a wire covered fence that just allowed us to touch each others' fingers in place of a handshake, a hug, or a kiss. My mother would cry and my father would talk to my brother in quiet, low tones while my eyes darted around the room at the other inmates and their families. Finally my brother would call my name and ask me about school or comment on what I was wearing. I don't remember what we actually talked about. I relished his attention, though I recall I was very shy around him.

My strongest memories are about how he looked, how he smiled when he saw us, how he looked straight at me when we talked, and how his face changed when we had to say good-bye. Even today I grow sad at what I missed in not having my only brother at home with me.

b Answer the questions on a separate sheet of paper.

1. What memories does the writer have of her brother before prison?
2. Why does she remember the sound of the electronic prison gates?
3. What process took place before the girl and her parents could see her brother?
4. How did the girl react to this process?
5. What things did the girl notice about her brother during the visits?

5 Find the underlined words or phrases in the story that mean:

1. loud noise ____________
2. prisoners ____________
3. being in prison ____________
4. be searched ____________
5. prison ____________
6. unclear ____________
7. can't remember ____________
8. walk proudly ____________
9. looked quickly ____________
10. enjoyed ____________

LESSON 2

Vocabulary

1 Add one word to complete each sentence.

1. We have volunteered help move people out of the disaster area.
2. Since the old manager left, the office has spiraled.
3. Unfortunately, the soccer player gave his wife of attorney, and she spent all the money.
4. The local farmers invested in the water company but never saw a of the profit that was made.
5. He was a media millionnaire, but after the scandal he bankruptcy.
6. Sam hasn't been able to work since the car accident, so he's going sue the other driver.

Grammar

2 Complete the sentences using the correct form of the verbs in parentheses.

1. If I ____________ my car here, I ____________ you a lift. (have) (offer)
2. If it ____________ for Jamie, we ____________ for a long time. (not be) (wait)
3. If you ____________ carefully to what I said, this ______________! (listen) (not happen)
4. Provided that she ____________ all the medications, she ____________ fine. (take) (be)
5. If only they ____________ us ten minutes earlier, we ______________ the order. (call) (cancel)
6. Unless Mr. Lee ____________ his strategy, the business ____________ bankrupt. (change) (go)
7. Should they happen ____________ her the job, would she ____________ it? (offer) (accept)

3 Complete the beginning of each sentence with the correct word. Then circle the correct ending.

1. ____________ that the team keeps playing as they are right now,
   a. we had a good chance of winning the cup.
   b. we have a good chance of winning the cup.
2. Should you ____________ to see Brad on your travels,
   a. could you tell him I've been trying to contact him?
   b. you could have told him I'd been trying to contact him.
3. If it ____________ been for Selena telling us,
   a. we never realized what they were planning.
   b. we never would have realized what they were planning.
4. If you ____________ like to see the rest of the house,
   a. I could have left the key, and you could show yourself around.
   b. I can leave you the key, and you can show yourself around.
5. If ____________ we hadn't bought the tickets already,
   a. then we could change our plans.
   b. then we changed our plans.
6. As ____________ as Sheila still works there,
   a. she should be able to give you all the information you need.
   b. she could be able to give you all the information you need.

Vocabulary

4 Complete the paragraph with words from the box.

generosity	lavishly	vision	deal
Foundation	inspired	impact	
admirable	dedicate	charity	
donating	fortune	mission	

Warren Buffet, the world's greatest stock market investor, announced he was giving away most of his $24 billion __________ (1.). The world's second richest man is __________ (2.) the money to the Bill and Melinda Gates __________ (3.), whose __________ (4.) is to tackle AIDS and global poverty. This is __________ (5.) on an industrial scale. The __________ (6.) of these two men will now far outstrip the contribution of most aid organizations to Africa. The domino effect could have an equally significant __________ (7.): if important role-models __________ (8.) a great __________ (9.) of their wealth to helping the poor and the sick, then perhaps others might be __________ (10.) to give away money rather than simply spend it __________ (11.) on themselves and their families. Two hundred years ago, William Blake argued that charity, however __________ (12.) on an individual level, is wrong because it delays reform and perpetuates economic injustice. Doubtless, many still agree with that view. But the sheer scale of the Gates–Buffett "mega-merger," and their joint __________ (13.) for a way towards a better future, is surely bad news for critics of the market system.

Reading

5a Read the article quickly. What is the significance of these numbers?

1. 64   2. 30s   3. 2.5 million   4. 80–100   5. 30   6. $103 million

Instant millionaires need help

1 The high-tech world is making thousands of very young people very rich, but according to psychologists, it is also creating a new illness—sudden-wealth syndrome.

2 Some seek help because they are too rich and cannot handle their wealth, others because they crave more money or feel guilty. Dr. Stephen Goldbart, a psychologist, runs the Money, Meaning & Choices Institute near Silicon Valley, where 64 new millionaires are reportedly created every day. Most of them are people in their 20s and 30s who find themselves suddenly rich, a group Dr. Goldbart calls the "Siliconaires."

3 He noticed a change several years ago, when people from middle-class backgrounds started coming into large sums of money. With the dot.com trend of recent years, his client numbers have steadily increased. In April, Merrill Lynch reported that the number of millionaires in the United States and Canada has risen almost 40% since 1997, to 2.5 million.

4 Becoming unexpectedly rich has its drawbacks, Dr. Goldbart says, and there should be some amount of sympathy for those who cannot handle sudden wealth. "It can ruin their lives, rip their families apart, and lead them on a path of destructive behavior," he says. "Money does not always bring peace and fulfillment. They lose balance. Instead of money solving all their problems, it often brings guilt, stress, and confusion."

5 People who are used to working 80 to 100 hours a week on their fledgling enterprise suddenly find they no longer need to work and are able to retire at the age of 30. However, the newfound leisure puts them into a premature mid-life crisis. Some experience panic attacks, severe depression, and insomnia, Dr. Goldbart says. Others withdraw from society or go on maniacal shopping sprees.

6 Some newly rich feel guilty about having so much money and feel they are not entitled to it, or that they do not deserve it. Others become paranoid, thinking they will be exploited because of their wealth, or they become obsessed with making even more money. People most affected are the "new rich," for whom wealth was not part of their upbringing and who expected to spend their lives working. Anxiety and depression can also come from "ticker shock" as they watch the vagaries in the stock market, particularly a plunge when they have not exercised their stock options.

7 Part of Dr. Goldbart's cure for the unhappy rich is to get them involved in the community and not just writing checks to charities. British Columbia's Rory Holland, executive vice-president of Itemus, made his millions when the company he was involved in for eight years was sold for $103 million in 1998. He now devotes much of his time to four non-profit groups, serves on their boards, and helps raise money.

8 Dr. Goldbart believes he is the only psychologist, along with family counselor Joan DiFuria, providing therapy for the rich, and would like to see more colleagues provide the service. "These people [the rich] are sensitive to how people feel and are reluctant to use our kind of service," he says. "But we help them regain the balance they've lost."

b Read the article again. Answer the questions on a separate sheet of paper.

1. What has caused the increase in the number of millionaires?
2. What feelings can people who come into sudden wealth experience? How can these feelings affect them?
3. Who might be particularly affected?
4. What might be the cause of these feelings?
5. What does Dr. Goldbart suggest as a cure?
6. How does Dr. Goldbart feel the public should treat sudden millionaires?

6 Complete the sentences with words or phrases from the article.

1. I have so much work at the moment, I just can't __________ it. (paragraph 2)
2. I've given up caffeine, but I still __________ coffee first thing in the morning. (paragraph 2)
3. For me, the advantages outweigh the __________ when you're living in a city like Bogota. (paragraph 4)
4. The effect of the earthquake was literally to __________ the whole community. (paragraph 4)
5. The plans aren't very advanced yet. It's just a __________ idea. (paragraph 5)
6. He's quit his job, taken up jogging, and started dance classes. I think he's having a __________. (paragraph 5)
7. She took all the credit for the ideas, even though she was not __________ to do so. (paragraph 6)
8. My father died when I was young, so we had a fairly difficult __________. (paragraph 6)

LESSON 3

Vocabulary

1 Complete the crossword.

Across

4. As a boss, he is very ____ of his employees.
5. I enjoy the ____ of working for myself.
6. The company invests in a private ____ plan on your behalf.
8. We get strange requests from our clients, so some of our tasks can be quite ____.
11. The employees received bonuses in recognition of their ____.
12. The number one ____ in this company is customer satisfaction.
13. The offices are modern and spacious, and there are lots of like-minded people, so it's a really good working ____.

Down

1. The pay is $39,000 a year, which is a good ____.
2. Abcom is a growing company, so there are plenty of ____ for promotion.
3. One of the best things about working here is the ____ of the location.
7. Most of the workers enjoyed a high degree of job ____.
9. We attend conferences and workshops as part of our professional ____.
10. It's a great job if you have children because of the ____ working hours.
12. Anyone can ____ an idea for improving the business.

2 Put the words in the correct order to make sentences.

1. for/work/is/to/walk/essential/to/me/able/the/thing/being

   ____

   ____________________.

2. opportunity/the/having/promotion/vital/is/for

   ____

   ____________________.

3. major/a/flexible/isn't/having/hours/priority/working

   ____

   ____________________.

4. job/is/main/priority/satisfaction/my

   ____

   ____________________.

5. couldn't/supportive/without/I/co-workers/do/job/my

   ____

   ____________________.

6. retirement/really/about/a/not/plan/I'm/having/concerned

   ____

   ____________________.

3 Complete the interview with words from the box.

plenty	little	deal	few	vast
handful	most	many	not	

Fun at Work

A: Crocodile curry and cheesy worms may not be everybody's idea of snack food, but MediaCom, rated number 28 in the *Sunday Times* listing of "Top 100 companies to work for," wants to encourage a creative and original take on the world. So, they offer chocolate ants to their workers at break times and have ____________ (1.) of other interesting ideas, too. With us this morning is Rachel Stanmore, a business expert who has spent some time in this innovative media company. And she's here to tell us more about it. Good morning, Rachel.

B: Good morning.

A: Now I'm ____________ (2.) much of an expert in these things, so tell me, Rachel, what the company's trying to achieve with these slightly strange ideas?

B: Well, the philosophy is that the company will do better if the workers are inspired. They don't want people coming to work thinking: "Oh, it's just another day at the office."

A: That's a pretty unusual philosophy.

B: Yes, only a ____________ (3.) of companies do this kind of thing.

A: Can you tell us a ____________ (4.) bit more about the company?

B: Sure. It's the UK's largest media agency, with 389 employees based in London and Edinburgh. The ____________ (5.) majority of the workers are young professionals, under 35, who may be earning a great ____________ (6.) of money, but more importantly, they like to feel appreciated and constantly motivated. For the ____________ (7.) part they are very supportive of the business, with as ____________ (8.) as eight out of ten employees feeling excited about where the company's going. And that's because they have control—they know what it's like to run things. Quite a ____________ (9.) of them have had their own ideas brought into operation. Last year, for example, there was a contest called "If I ran the company," and as a result, a company café was introduced, which provides free breakfasts in the morning, is open until 11:30 at night, and has the boss working behind it.

A: Not bad!

4 Read the interview again and answer the questions on a separate sheet of paper.

1. What is Rachel Stanmore's job?
2. What kind of company is MediaCom?

Grammar

5 Rewrite the sentences using the words in parentheses.

Ex: There is nothing we can do to stop the project. (seemingly)
There is seemingly nothing we can do to stop the project.

1. You may be surprised to hear that sales figures were up from last year. (believe)
____
____
2. Everyone says that the company is losing a lot of money. (apparently)
____
____
3. For the most part, the management team has a good relationship with the rest of the employees. (broadly)
____
____
4. In my opinion, the conclusions of the report are wrong. (fundamentally)
____
____
5. I'd like to say no to the extra work, but I need the money. (hand)
____
____
6. What you say is true, but only in part. (point)
____
____
7. I travel a lot for my job. On the whole, I enjoy it, although it can be exhausting. (large)
____
____
8. Looking back, we probably should have approached them earlier. (in)
____
____
9. Unexpectedly, the results of the survey indicate that there could be a good market for the new product. (enough)
____
____

UNIT 5
Review

1 Match the beginning of the sentence with its end.

____ 1. She hasn't had to worry about money since they sold the business and she came
____ 2. We are paid a fixed salary, plus a 10%
____ 3. He managed to bring the price down by
____ 4 His business went
____ 5. If you know what you are doing, there is plenty of money
____ 6. The house is filled with priceless
____ 7. Ana has worked hard and deserves a

a. bankrupt a few years ago.
b. paintings.
c. commission.
d. raise.
e. to be made on the stock market.
f. into a fortune.
g. haggling with the owner.

2 Complete each sentence by adding a word from the box.

don't	would	you	as	only	for

1. If it hadn't been the weather, we would have had a wonderful vacation.
2. You can use my phone, provided that you talk for too long.
3. If I had listened to her advice!
4. Should happen to be in Mexico City, you should call my sister.
5. If you let us know as soon as the package arrives, that would be great.
6. As long he lives in that house, I'm not going back there.

3 Choose the correct words to complete each sentence.

1. What ____ when she told us there was no alternative?
   a. she did mean
   b. she means
   c. did she mean
2. I ____ him take the money.
   a. actually saw
   b. saw actually
   c. actual saw
3. They were so relieved to finally buy ____ house.
   a. their own
   b. on their own
   c. own their
4. The journey was ____.
   a. by means no easy
   b. by no means easy
   c. no means by easy
5. ____ impresses me about them is that they are so efficient.
   a. The most thing that
   b. The thing that most
   c. Most the thing that
6. He's not ____.
   a. interested all at soccer
   b. interested in soccer all at
   c. interested in soccer at all

4 Use the clues to complete the crossword.

Across

4. Their ____ was to help the homeless.
6. They spend a ____ on childcare so that they can both go to work.
7. The changes have definitely had a major ____.
11. Take a look at their ____ illustrated catalog.
12. Don't eat any more. You're just being ____.

Down

1. She enjoys ____ money to a good cause.
2. Our ____ is to expand the business over the next five years.
3. Her work has ____ others to join the profession.
5. A wage of $175 a week is hardly enough to ____ for a growing family.
6. The organization was ____ in the mid-1990s.
8. He ____ most of the money into a high-interest bank account.
9. I give all my old clothes to ____.
10. The government has spent a great ____ of money on renovating the old buildings.

5 Complete the sentences using the correct form of the words in parentheses.

1. My work gives me a lot of job ______________. (satisfy)
2. Luckily, my boss is very ______________. (support)
3. The pay isn't very good initially, but there are good opportunities for ______________. (promote)
4. Working under deadlines can be quite ______________. (challenge)
5. The company helps with your professional ______________. (develop)
6. Having worked at night for so long, it is great to have such ______________ working hours. (flex)
7. One of the benefits of the apartment is its ______________ location. (convenient)

6 Cross out the choices that are NOT possible, or have a different meaning.

1. We try to support each other, and ____ it seems to work.
   a. by and large
   b. however
   c. broadly speaking
2. Transcil always deals with the problem quickly. ____, they do charge a lot for their services.
   a. Essentially
   b. On the other hand
   c. However
3. We cut our prices by nearly 50%, and ____ we managed to increase our profits.
   a. believe it or not
   b. surprisingly enough
   c. in hindsight
4. She is working for herself and ____ doing very well.
   a. on the other hand
   b. apparently
   c. seemingly
5. The business is ____ a technical marketing company.
   a. essentially
   b. looking back
   c. fundamentally
6. They moved the factory to China to cut costs. ____, it was the right decision.
   a. In hindsight
   b. Looking back
   c. However

English in Common **ActiveBook**
Installation Instructions

Windows

- Insert the disc into the CD-ROM drive of your computer. On most computers, the program will begin automatically.
- If the program does not begin automatically, open "My Computer."
- Right-click on the CD-ROM icon. Click on Open.

Macintosh

- Insert the disc into the CD-ROM drive of your computer.
- Double-click on the CD-ROM icon on your desktop.
- Double click on the "START_OSX" file to run the program. Leave the CD-ROM in the computer while using the program.

Note: You must have administrator privileges on the computer to install the program. To install:

- **Windows:** Double-click on the "install" file to start the installation.
- **Macintosh:** Copy all files from the CD-ROM to a folder on your hard drive.

ActiveBook System Requirements

	PC Compatible	**Macintosh Compatible**
Operating System	Microsoft Windows® XP, Vista, Windows 7	Mac OSX v. (10.4 & 10.5)
Processor	Intel Pentium® IV 1000MHz or faster processor (or equivalent)	PowerPC & Intel processor 500MHz or faster processor (or equivalent)
RAM	512 MB RAM minimum or higher	512 MB RAM minimum or higher
Internet Browser	Microsoft Internet Explorer® 7.x or Mozilla Firefox™ 4.x, or higher	Safari® 3.x, Mozilla Firefox™ 4.x, or higher
Plug-ins	Adobe PDF 8, Adobe Flash 9, or higher	Adobe PDF 8, Adobe Flash 9, or higher
Hardware	Computer CD-ROM drive, sound card and speakers or headphones	Computer CD-ROM drive, sound card and speakers or headphones
Monitor Resolution	1024x768	1024x768
Internet Connection	DSL, cable/broadband, T1, or other high-speed connection required to download plug-ins	

TECHNICAL SUPPORT

For Technical Product Support, please visit our support website at www.PearsonLongmanSupport.com. You can search our *Knowledgebase* for frequently asked questions, instantly *Chat* with an available support representative, or *Submit a Ticket/Request* for assistance.